From Doodlebugs to Devon

Sarah O Shaw

Published by Sarah Shaw, 2023.

FROM DOODLEBUGS TO DEVON

First edition. June 30, 2023.

Copyright © 2023 Sarah O Shaw.

ISBN: 979-8223341840

Written by Sarah O Shaw.

Table of Contents

For Mary and John

From Doodlebugs to Devon

Introduction

Imagine this: you're in south London in the summer of 1944, let's say planting potatoes on your allotment, making raspberry jam on the stove or washing dishes at the kitchen sink; or perhaps it's night time and you are lying on a camp bed inside a metal air-raid shelter in the pitch dark of the blackout. You hear a sound. One you have never heard before. It's a strange, sinister droning, a throbbing engine that gets louder and louder and louder until it stops.

There is complete silence.

And then, a huge explosion.

That was the experience of thousands of people who came under fire from flying bombs in the final year of the Second World War. Doodlebugs, as they were popularly known, were the first of two deadly weapons Hitler was convinced would win him the war. They were also the forerunners of today's guided missiles.

Many years ago, I acquired a collection of letters written from April 1944 to July 1945 by my mother to my father. She was a housewife in south London, he was an army officer in Scotland. As none of his letters survive it is a one-sided conversation, nevertheless, hers were fascinating. At first they tell of her relatively comfortable wartime life as she copes on a limited budget with restrictions and shortages while caring for her young son. Then, dramatically, the flying bombs appear. She endures their onslaught for several weeks before escaping to safety in Devon, but even there her troubles are not over. As a voluntary evacuee she is obliged to move from one lodging to another before eventually settling down to see out the war.

As Laura Cumming wrote in *On Chapel Sands,* 'the lives of our parents before we are born are the first great mystery'. My mother's letters raised all sorts of questions: What was it really like to live through those raids? Was her experience typical of others? Was there any truth in the rumour that the government had deliberately placed Croydon, the borough most hit by flying bombs, in the firing line? Why had she kept a photo of a group of Nazis? What was my father doing in Scotland, and why didn't he want her to join him there? For the answers, I turned to newspapers, books, local history societies and papers in the National and Parliamentary Archives, and discovered some extraordinary stories.

The German V-weapon campaign, 'Rumpelkammer' or Junkyard, has been written about from a variety of perspectives. British wartime propaganda stressed the resilience of civilians under fire. Military historians have viewed it much as the Chiefs of Staff did at the time: as a distraction from the immense war effort taking place on the continent of Europe and in the Pacific; while social historians tend to see it as yet another trial for those on the Home Front.

This book takes a different approach. It takes one woman's letters and explores them, using historical evidence to to show the impact of events and decisions on one individual, thereby creating an account that both confirms and challenges common perceptions of this period. Anyone with an interest in the Home Front during World War Two or whose family lived through those difficult days will find this book of interest.

As a disclaimer, I should add that I am not an academic, but have endeavoured to ensure the results of my research are presented as accurately as possible although, to fill in a few gaps, I have invented scenes based on other letters and family memories.

My mother, Yvonne Shaw, was an 'ordinary' woman living in extraordinary times. Although hers is a unique voice: brave, honest and funny, she speaks for the thousands of British housewives whose quiet resolve and good humour helped the Allies win the war.

Yvonne in 1939

The Family in 1944

Yvonne Shaw (nee Etheridge), b.1911, married Clement Shaw in 1939.

Their son, Oliver Shaw, b.1941.

Her mother, Dorothy Mabey, b.1885, married Charles Mabey in 1944.

Previously married to Frederic Ledger Etheridge (Yvonne & Rupert's father) who died in 1940.

Her brother, Rupert Ledger Etheridge, b.1909, married Suzanne (nee Cumby) in 1934.

Their children, Jennifer Ledger Etheridge, b.1936 and Michael Ledger Etheridge, b.1944.

Her maternal uncles:

(George) Dudley Brown, b.1882, married to Florence (nee Hayson)

Bernard Brown, b.1889, married Doris (nee Cortazzi).

Her maternal grandfather, George Frederick Brown, b. 1854.

Chapter 1
April to May 1944

'Seeing as how you have given the best years of your wife to the army...'

April 1st 1944: Saturday evening, All Fools' Day.

In the privet-lined streets of Purley, south of Croydon, south of London, the day is fading to twilight. A few minutes' walk from the railway station is Dale Road, a street lined with identical houses, each with a bay window and a neat front garden.

Apart from one exception.

Halfway down, as the road curves, stands a large red-brick villa. At the end of a gravel path is a white, wooden porch which gleams gently in the dusk, while on the upper floor steep gables rise above the windows like quizzical eyebrows. Beyond the house a lawn, dotted with flower beds, stretches away to a distant copse of trees.

This house was built in the 1890s to be the home of a self-made man and his family. Here, visitors would be ushered into lofty reception rooms while servants scurried in the awkward, chilly kitchens at the rear. But today, in the fifth year of the war, things are very different. Tonight the house conceals itself. Its windows are covered with blinds and thick cotton cloth to prevent light from escaping. Foxley Lodge is hiding from German airplanes.

Inside, sitting at an oak dining table in one of the front rooms, is
Yvonne Shaw. Nearly 33 years old, her fine, light-brown hair falls into
curls around her round, pleasant face. She's had a tiring day as usual,
shopping, cooking and looking after her four-year-old son. Now, while
he is asleep in the next room, she is relaxing, reading today's *Daily Mail*
and finishing a small cup of Camp coffee. She takes a silver cigarette
case from her handbag, her third cigarette of the day and her last
until more come on sale at the tobacconist's. Anyway, she thinks,
moderation in all things. She lights up and, as she exhales, her startling
blue eyes glance upwards with a look that is almost pleading. She
pauses, listening for sounds from the next room where her little boy,
Oliver, is sleeping, or from the floor above, or for the distant wail of an
air-raid siren. But all is quiet.

Yvonne trawls through the *Mail*. In Los Angeles, Charlie Chaplin has
been accused of transporting an actress across a state frontier for an
immoral purpose; in Portsmouth, a Scottish woman, guided by the
spirit of a deceased Dundee pattern maker, has been found guilty of
witchcraft. Tomorrow morning, she notes, she must move the clocks
forward one hour for Double Summer Time, and the blackout has to
remain in place until five minutes past seven. Further cuts to rations
are coming: coal down to four hundredweight a month while there
is precious little coke to be had, cheese reduced from three to two
ounces per person per week, scarcely enough for a mouse, she thinks.
Popular author H.G. Wells is 'ill but not in bed,' and 10,000 woollen
blankets, surplus to government requirements, have been released for
sale. Yvonne wonders whether Wells might appreciate one of them
when he does retire to bed; in fact, she would like one herself at the
moment, given how cold it is in this high-ceilinged room which the
little fire in the hearth is struggling to heat.

A particular announcement catches her eye. From tomorrow, members of the public are banned from travelling to all coastal areas south of a line drawn from the Wash to Land's End. This must be because plans for the much-anticipated Allied invasion of France are nearly ready. Further down the paragraph she finds something of even greater interest—the news that the same ban applies to parts of Scotland too, one of which is Stirling. And apparently here, the wives of men in the forces are still allowed to visit their husbands.

Yvonne gazes at the empty chair opposite. A few days ago, her tall, handsome, sensitive husband had been sitting there, and already those days feel as if they belong to another world. It had been such a joyful reunion, little Oliver's Daddy showing him how to hold a cricket bat, reading books to him, the three of them taking walks together and having fun unpacking when Clem's few remaining possessions came out of storage and joined all the other odds and ends in what is called The Muck Room.

Now that all service leave has been cancelled, goodness knows how long it will be before she sees him again. But does this allowance for wives to visit Scotland mean she might be able to go to Stirling and they 'will meet again,' as the syrupy Vera Lynn song they both detest so much puts it?

She had always known when she married Clem at the outbreak of war that it would be difficult to maintain their marriage when they had to rely on letters, infrequent phone calls and the occasional week's leave to keep in touch. Her attention was necessarily focussed on the daily grind of providing for her son and herself and keeping their home going. During the war, consumer goods were largely controlled by the government through two systems: essential food items and clothing were rationed by coupons and registration with local shops; other items, such as tinned goods and biscuits, were limited by a 'points' system which varied according to what was available and in demand. As a result, a few days ago she had found herself having to persuade Oliver that Hasty Pudding (a concoction of oatmeal, suet and a parsnip) with gravy was the lunch of heroes. And all the while mindful that there might be another bombing raid that night. It was a challenge every housewife had to face.

Yvonne decides she must tell Clem about the shotgun and the bed. She pushes the newspaper aside and looks in the sideboard for writing paper. There is none. Another wartime shortage. Instead, she finds a pile of blank receipts from her late father's dentistry practice and, holding a Bakelite pen in her left hand and dipping it into a bottle of Quink ink, uses them.

1st April, Saturday eve

Dear darling,

Thank you for the letter.

I sold your shotgun for £5 this evening, as advertised. So here is a cheque therefore. At least you can buy yourself a new mac. with the proceeds. The purchaser, by the way, was one of the new rich, a self-assured youth of about sixteen with much oil on the head and a cigarette stuck permanently on the lower lip. He earns probably about £8 a week and addressed me as if I were a sort of char. He wanted it for a holiday in Devon and dithered a bit because he said there weren't very many cartridges and you couldn't buy them now. However, I left him to it and after a few stray shots at the neighbours he asked me to wrap it up in newspaper "so the cops wouldn't spot it".

There has only been one enquiry for the bed, "£40 in perfect condition", but the poor old dear didn't read the ad. very carefully and thought it was going for £10, or so she said. She pitched a long sad story about being bombed out from Addiscombe last week and no furniture saved, but of course I remained stony-hearted and didn't budge a bob. I don't actually think we should get £40 now. I had a good look at the bed this afternoon, the headboard is badly scratched and the mattress isn't exactly clean. However, maybe we shall be glad to swap it for a couple of tins of spam in 1950. Don't let's sell the billiard table either. It won't be long before Oliver will be able to get some fun out of it and it doesn't take up much space in the Muck Room.

Glad you are pleased with the way our poppet is growing up. If only his bright eyes and pink cheeks outlast the war I shall be content with my war work. The latest accomplishment is to make quite eatable toast—slightly smoky I must admit—but I eat it with exclamations of delight.

"Did you hear all those bombers going over last night?" he gravely asked today.

Pause.

Then, "What is bombers, mummie?"

We've been left alone by the Luftwaffe since you went back due, as everyone seems to think, to the moon. The Friday raid was really very bad in South Croydon, hundreds of incendiaries around Croham Park. Mother's solicitor, Dinn, was completely burnt out. He said the fire engines were summoned from the other side of London but the nozzles of their pumps wouldn't fit the local mains and they had to stand by helpless.

Awfully sorry you are getting such mouldy food slapped at you. What a pity there isn't a decent mess in the neighbourhood. I'm sure the army is getting better stuff than the civilian establishments.

I've been eating my way thru cold pork all the week, only to be told today that I should have to have it again. Whereupon I practically wept aloud and told them that it was time my child ceased being a vegetarian and the butcher, viewing the moist sawdust around my feet, dived into the strong room and returned bearing aloft a peculiar piece of beef called, I believe, top of the round—the sort of thing you wouldn't look at in 1939—but anyway I can stew it and Oliver can live on the gravy. I also managed to amass 4 lbs of oranges from our black marketeers so life has its brighter moments. Just had a look round the larder to see if I could send you anything. Could you do with a tin of blackcurrant purée? Very good for the complexion. If you don't get any fruit, couldn't you buy yourself a lettuce occasionally?

Dear me, how the woman does run on. You might think she cared tuppence about you which is, as Pythagoras would say, absurd.

The lush and futile one. xx

Yvonne blots the letter, puts it in an envelope addressed to Captain C.L. Shaw at the Golden Lion Hotel, Stirling, Scotland, sticks a blue tuppence-ha'penny stamp on it and leaves it on the table to be posted tomorrow.

The 'Friday raid on March 24th', happened before the end of Clem's leave. The bombs caused significant damage to areas between Purley and its larger neighbour to the north, Croydon. It was part of what became known as the 'Little Blitz', an unwelcome resumption of attacks on London after a period of quiet following the main Blitz of 1940–41.

There's more than a whiff of middle-class snobbery in Yvonne's attitude to the 'new rich' and the 'poor old dear' who responded to her advertisements, but this attitude wasn't unusual. While British propaganda stressed that the people, rich, poor and everything in between, were united in pursuit of victory, class prejudice was still part of normal society. But why was she so stony-hearted about the bed, especially as the woman had come four miles to look at it? Perhaps Clem had told her it was worth £40 and she loyally stuck to the amount even if, as is quite possible, he made up the figure on the spur of the moment. Or perhaps their income was much less than living in a house the size of Foxley Lodge would suggest; Yvonne's mother was already paying the rates on it and Clem's army salary didn't bring in much. Whatever the reason, the bed now disappears from view. The billiard table met a sad end a few years later when it was found to be full of woodworm and burned on a bonfire.

As for the black-market oranges, Allied victories in North Africa had allowed them to be imported into Britain again, hence the four pounds in Yvonne's shopping basket.[1] There was great excitement about their arrival on sale. Diarist Vere Hodgson recorded how a greengrocer had to push his way through an eager queue to get into his own shop.[2] Yvonne bought hers illegally because the government had recently reduced their price and wholesalers promptly withdrew the fruit from sale to the shops. Instead the supply was diverted to black-market dealers where greater profits were guaranteed.

Next day, Yvonne and Oliver walk up Dale Road to the Godstone Road and turn left towards a small parade of shops. Being a Sunday, they are all shut and their blinds drawn down. She hands the envelope to her little boy and lifts him up. 'Post this to Daddy,' she says, and he drops the letter into its red, rectangular mouth. 'I heard it fall, Mummie,' he cries, as she lowers him to the pavement.

They walk back holding hands, Oliver skipping and tugging, Yvonne wondering whether offering Clem the blackcurrant purée was a good idea or whether he will be annoyed by her fussing. It's so difficult to know what is the right thing to say when your husband is away for so long and is sometimes apt to get the wrong end of the stick. She wonders whether he will be mollified by her quoting back to him what he called her last week. Well, the letter has gone now, so it's too late to worry.

Instead of speculating about the future, she must consider what to cook for lunch. The best thing to do with that 'top of the round,' she decides, is to stew it with potatoes, a couple of turnips and one of her precious onions. The oranges can come afterwards. She looks down at her son, dark-haired, and with a round face so like her own, and vows that when the war is over she will buy him a very large ice cream, one made with real cream and eggs.

They are back home again. As they open the front door, Jennie, Yvonne's lively eight-year-old niece, dances down the stairs singing her favourite song, 'Whistle while you work,' completely out of tune. Behind her, her mother, Suzanne, descends with the slow and careful tread of a small and heavily pregnant woman. Her approach, as always, is signalled by the sound of clinking bracelets and a loud, nasal 'hello'.

Foxley Lodge had indeed been acquired in the early 1900s by a self-made man: Yvonne's father. He had used it as both his family home and as the site of one of his two dental practices, the other one being in Hanover Square. On his death in 1940, the house was divided between Yvonne on the ground floor, and her elder brother Rupert, whose wife and daughter live upstairs. Rupert, having followed his father into dentistry, is now in the RAF in Manchester, drilling and filling the teeth of The Few.

The women discuss their plans for the day while Jennie spirits Oliver outside to the sandpit to play Soldiers in the Desert. Only ten minutes away, trucks full of real soldiers head down the Brighton Road to the coast and depots crammed with tanks, aircraft, ships and planes. In the south west, troops are wading through waves and climbing cliffs rehearsing for the largest seaborne invasion in history. In London, Generals Montgomery and Eisenhower and their staff pore over maps, reconnaissance photos and intelligence reports; and all around the country warehousemen, accountants, camouflage artists, seamstresses, ammunition manufacturers, railwaymen and typists are hard at work.

Yvonne's letter waits in the post box to be collected and to make its journey north.

Clem

With the huge military preparations taking place, what was Clem doing in Scotland? It had always been a mystery to me because, although he often talked about Stirling Castle and the 'Jocks' with whom he served, he never mentioned what his actual duties had been. I grew up believing he must have been involved in secret missions and imagined him buried in a hayloft somewhere with a transmitter, tapping out messages in Morse Code; or lying in the heather, scanning the purple glen through a pair of binoculars. Both of these seemed plausible when, in the late 1950s, he took out of the loft at Foxley

Lodge a mysterious pile of maps and documents with curious markings on them and burned them in the garden, bonfires being very much a feature of suburban family life. When I asked him why he was doing this, he answered, 'Because they could still be of use to the enemy.' 'Why? What were you doing?' I asked. He said casually, 'Oh, defending Scotland against a German invasion.'

A few years ago, I obtained his Army Record and discovered that his regiment was the Royal Scots Fusiliers, which explained his connection to Scotland. It turned out that after training he was sent to France as a junior officer in the not exactly glamorous Pioneer Corps, escaped the Blitzkrieg (no, not from Dunkirk but from Cherbourg) and then went to Frinton to organise the building of pillboxes in case of a German invasion. In 1943, he was posted to Scotland with the rank of Captain.

So far, so good. But to find out more, one damp December day I went to the National Archives in Kew, having called up about a dozen boxes of records. Nearly all the files had intriguingly missing pages, but from what was left I was able to piece together something about what Clem had been up to, thus shedding a glimmer of light into a dusty corner of Second World War history.

Clem was a staff officer in the Eastern Division of Scotland working with the Home Guard, the 'Dad's Army' of volunteers who were either too old or too young to serve in the regular forces or who were employed in reserved occupations like farming and shipbuilding. The most sensitive military site in his area was the Royal Dockyard at Rosyth on the Firth of Forth, where the navy refitted and repaired some of its warships. Clem's role was to help organise training and exercises so the men would be able to defend against any attacks on the area, especially on the dockyard.

In April 1944, around the time that Yvonne's first letter was written, Clem wrote a memo dated April 15th addressed to the Divisional HQ and marked 'Important' and 'Secret', with the promising instruction, 'If liable to be intercepted or to fall into enemy hands, this message must be sent IN CIPHER.'

It was a lengthy document listing Clem's concerns about a forthcoming 'Exercise Umbrella', a practice against any attack on the dockyard by an 'enemy agent.' The Home Guard brigades were to recapture the area and other strategic points, and assist the police in apprehending the supposed 'agent'. However, it seems Clem has come into this plan part way through. He is very agitated because he thinks there isn't enough time to make the necessary arrangements and organise the men. Moreover, local employers are unlikely to release enough men for the exercise. Clearly irritated by an apparent lack of forethought by the higher ranks, he asks what he should do if any men refuse to turn out. Will the army offer compensation to volunteers who lose pay for taking part in the exercise? And if not enough Home Guard men are available, has he permission to bring in a troop of Polish soldiers? He ends the memo with 'I have called a conference of HG [Home Guard] for 1100 hrs for 16 Apr. May I have your answer by then?'[3] The reply, which comes from a Lt Col Reed, dismisses Clem's concerns completely. All the necessary details are covered in another document, which presumably Clem hasn't seen, and 'Full information will be given to your senior officer at the meeting of Scottish Command tomorrow. It is understood that very few Home Guard will be affected in your Sub-District.'[4]

Well, that looks like a slapdown. I imagine Clem was pretty miffed, having expressed what he thought were genuine concerns. Perhaps the fact that these papers are still in the file suggests that the Exercise Umbrella wasn't quite as Important and Secret as Clem had thought.

The following day, normal army business resumes. Clem receives two messages. The first orders him to train a Home Guard battalion for rescue work, to replace already trained men who are needed in the south to deal with any German counter-attacks after the Allied invasion.[5] The second instructs him that, in the case of an air raid, the Home Guard may now use 'not only sirens, but rattles, handbells, whistles, strombon horns' [a klaxon which can be heard three to four miles away] and even, 'the use of a bugler in a car... for the purpose of raising a <u>localised</u> alarm.'[6] It's all a long way from clandestine Morse Code signals and binoculars in the heather, but in total war everyone played their part.

Yvonne's next letter to Clem refers to her mother, Dorothy, a bright, kindly and intelligent woman. Born in 1885, she had married Yvonne's father, who was 15 years older than her, in 1908. He had died of pneumonia in 1940. Dorothy married again a few weeks before Yvonne's first letter, this time to a family friend and wealthy, well-connected widower, Charles Mabey. They were living in a flat near Flood Street in Chelsea. Charles had retired from a successful career as London agent for the Cambridge Street India Rubber Works, which advertised itself as making waterproof clothing. Useful as these garments were, Dorothy and Yvonne were privately amused that the company's principle profits came from the sale of a more widely used rubber product.

Dorothy, a former suffragist, remained concerned about women's lives. For example, in January 1939 she wrote a strongly worded letter to the local newspaper under the alluring heading, 'Purley—a place in which to die'. She described the social isolation of young mothers and wives of 'invalids and the unemployed' in Purley's 'small houses', by which she probably meant smaller than Foxley Lodge, who were unable to afford the kind of domestic help she had been able to employ herself while her children were growing up. These young women were unable to go to church with their children and make new friends because, in the absence of a cook, they had to stay at home and cook the Sunday dinner. They couldn't go out in the evenings with their husbands either, because there was no one at home to look after the children or, if left by themselves, they would become 'terror-stricken.'

Dorothy offered solutions. 'I would like to see ... cafes run on Continental lines where, for the price of a cup of coffee or a glass of beer, a man could spend hours with his wife and children,' and, anticipating the rise of babysitting circles, she also recommended that a 'band of women' be formed 'who would give time to minding children and invalids in the evenings.'[7] Of course, in the following few months the likelihood of war put a stop to any general concerns about the plight of isolated women—although an outraged reader, signing herself 'Domestic' replied to Dorothy's letter asking why servants shouldn't be able to go to church as well.

Yvonne's next letter brings not only Dorothy to our attention, but also a small newcomer to Foxley Lodge.

Thursday, 13th April

Dearest darling,

Hectic days. Suzanne's boy arrived at ten yesterday morning and ever since I've been up in the air with callers, phone and so forth. We walked up the road together in the middle of the night, 4 pm to be exact, poor Suzanne having to stop and lean on every other gate post.

I couldn't sleep after that, and when the good news came through I felt almost as if I'd had a hand in the proceedings myself. It's a whopping child, 9 lbs, not bad for wartime, is it? He has lots of black long hair and looks very like Scrupe

[Rupert] and Jennie. I was allowed a couple of minutes with them both in the afternoon. Suzanne is terribly bucked at getting the family balanced and disproving her wretched doctor's prophesy that it was bound to be a girl. The only disappointment is that Scrupe won't get his leave, not even on compassionate grounds. Jennie is a bit glum as she wanted a sister but I keep cracking up the advantages of being the only girl.

The blooming siren started up last night just as I got the kids tucked up in the shelter, Oliver still asleep, and then a couple of neighbours rattled the letter box and wanted to know if I minded being alone. Very nice of them but I'd much rather be on my own than have to make polite conversation when feeling half dead. Oliver woke up for the all clear so we all three tucked up together and slept until 8 this morning. Jennie is going to continue to sleep with me while Suzanne is away as she is a bit nervous at night.

Mother came down today and took us out to lunch at Wilson's coffee house. I think the marriage is a success, at any rate judging from her. She already looks ten years younger and seems awfully happy.

Don't expect much in the way of letters for the next three weeks as I shall have rather a lot to do. Apart from the two kids, there will be all Suzanne's visitors who will probably look in here on the way. Joy is spending Friday night here. She is in town for two weeks, having left her two children at Budleigh.

Have been working in the garden quite a bit in the evenings, now that they are lighter. Most of the spade work is done and I've cut all the grass twice. My mower is so much lighter than mother's and doesn't tire me at all. Luckily I bought it in Caterham while you were in France. Put in a lot of lettuces which look like growing up.

Blooming man still hasn't been in to see about the wireless but I've got past missing it and can always hop upstairs for the news.

Sorry to have to report that the deal for the gun was a flop. He brought it back last week and wanted his money back as he had been pinched by a policeman trying it in his garden. You see, you do need a licence for it. I had told him I didn't think it was necessary as I hadn't seen one about. Anyway apparently there is great difficulty getting one now and so I gave him back the £5, I couldn't bothered to argue. I don't think we had better try to sell it again, not while the war is on. Perhaps you could find out first whether it is legal to own such things now.

Hoped to have the photos to send you this week but, like everything else, they take an age to get done.

Oliver has gone into pyjamas and struts around very proudly, the only trouble being that they won't stay up, the trouser part I mean.

Half asleep. Does this letter make sense?

Loving thoughts from your red hot Mom.

Where were the two women going when they went 'up the road' together? Where was the baby born? Purley Hospital is in the opposite direction and would have been a long, difficult walk for a woman in labour. There is a clue in an old family photograph album: a postcard announcing Oliver's birth, which shows the silhouette of a man running up a street with a stork flying above him, carrying in its beak a baby wrapped in a shawl. They are heading to the Homeside Nursing Home which, it turned out, was at the other end of Dale Road.

One advantage of living in Foxley Lodge was the sizeable garden, providing plenty of space to grow fruit and vegetables. At the end of the group of trees and furthest from the house, half-buried in Purley's clay soil, stood the family's Anderson shelter, a semi-circular, galvanised steel hobbit home covered with earth, inside which up to six people could fit if they squashed up together. It had to be aired and heated every night to be comfortable to sleep in, but served its purpose in protecting them from bombs, though not from a direct hit.

It's not clear whether Dorothy's visit was the first since her new marriage, but she must have been delighted to meet her third grandchild. Oliver would have enjoyed the visit to Wilson's Coffee House, especially if she bought him a little Kunzel cake, made from substitute chocolate, non-egg sponge cake and margarine icing. There were advantages to the arrival of a cousin.

Suzanne and Rupert with baby Michael

On Monday April 23rd, back in Chelsea, Dorothy wrote to her daughter, having done what good grandmothers do and taken out insurance policies for her two grandsons; although not, it seems, for Jennie. It's a curious letter, which suggests that thinking about the future of her grandchildren has led her back to depression, a condition which haunted her all her life.

Darling,

I am leaving Oliver a bit in my will, but I am just arranging to pay an Insurance Policy for him which will bring in about £90 spread over 3 years when he is 17, 18, 19. It isn't much but I am hoping he will be good at continental languages and will spend the money on holidays abroad. I expect I will be departed this life by then. I shall be perhaps forgotten by him. He has been such a joy to me, I want him to enjoy life and always look after you.

Lovingly,

Mother.

Next day is sunny and dry. Suzanne has gone away with the baby, now named Michael, probably to visit her parents, leaving Jennie in Yvonne's care. With both children finally in bed, Yvonne unwinds with a cigarette and newspaper before settling down to write to Clem.

Tuesday, 25th April, 10.30 pm.

Dearest darling,

Quite a time, I know, since I last wrote but I'm about as much stuck for something to say as you are. I am enjoying my foster-motherhood and shall be quite sorry when Jennie goes upstairs again, although of course it will be rather nice to have Oliver all to myself at times. Suzanne is coming back next Sunday and Jennie starts her new school on the Wednesday.

Had a hectic weekend. Discovered a burst pipe on Saturday evening, too late to get the plumbers. This meant turning the water off at the mains and letting the tanks run dry, rushing upstairs to fill saucepans and kettles from the bath all Sunday. Still, we survived and all is now repaired. It turned out to be two bursts: one from the upstairs bathroom hot pipe and one from the cold underneath the wash basin, so that the drips came through the passage by the scullery door.

Joy came to stay on Friday for three days, and she didn't bring a scrap of rations! We had a nice afternoon out on Saturday at Merstham, did our usual walk to see the cows and then over the hill by the cricket pitch and tea at the Golden Wheel. It was simply boiling, and so was Sunday, which we spent in deck chairs in the garden except for the usual tear up the road to watch the band[8]

Joy is now in a large furnished house in Budleigh Salterton, sharing it with an officer in the Marines and his wife. Stinking nuisance about the travel ban, otherwise Oliver and I could have a buckshee holiday there. I somehow don't think it will be lifted this summer, even if the boating party comes off next month, do you? The noise overhead down here is pretty big in the daytime now. We seem to be working up to something terrific quite soon, eh what?

Am taking the children on Friday to the Grand to see a dancing display by local kids. I did think *Snow White* might be a good idea until I saw a crowd of about two hundred waiting for the next performance on Monday.

Poor Oliver had a bad day today. First he scribbled all over the nursery door in green chalk and indelible pencil, then a scene at dinner because he didn't like the brown top to the fish pie. Finally he upset a pail full of water over the bathroom floor. The water came dripping into the downstairs lav where I was comfortably installed and, of course, I immediately thought "another bloody burst pipe", and phoned the plumbers! However, he has promised to be extra specially good tomorrow. I wonder.

A note from Mother yesterday to say that she is taking out a small insurance policy which will bring in Oliver about £100 over three years when he is 17, 18 and 19. She wants him to use the money on holidays abroad so that he will be able to climb mountains and love them as much as she does. A marvellous idea, don't you think?

I suppose the ban on leave will make yours considerably later than three months, even if it is lifted then. Still, it's no good worrying and we were lucky to get it in first before. "Your turn next", everyone blithely says, and I must admit I am more than a bit envious and would like to be Suzanne up the road just now. How about it?

Love, Y.

Poor Oliver. Obliged to share his mother's attention with both his lively older cousin and one of her best friends, it's no wonder he took to scrawling graffiti on the nursery door.

At a time of rationing, visiting without bringing your own share of food was considered poor etiquette. Yvonne's personal allowance for the week would have been 2oz butter, 2oz cheese, 4oz margarine, 2oz of tea, one fresh egg and three pints of milk. It didn't stretch far. She was able to grow some fruit and vegetables in the garden to make up for the any shortages but otherwise, she would have had to make do with whatever was in the larder (there was no fridge). Perhaps the blackcurrant jam saved the day? Somehow she managed, and her hospitality was rewarded later on, as we shall see.

It wasn't just food that was restricted. There were shortages of other things too, like socks, sheets, safety pins, shoe laces, sanitary towels, soap, string, cardboard, matches and detergents. In her novel, *The Two Mrs Abbotts,* published in 1943, D.E. Stevenson describes how a mother takes her two children shopping to buy a present for their nurse. They agree they can't buy her a dressing-gown, bedroom slippers or a box of chocolates as they don't have enough coupons. When they reach the shops they notice that, while the shelves don't look empty, it's because they are full of things that nobody wants. Eventually, at a general store they ask in turn for a fountain pen, a small clock, nail scissors, a bedside lamp or a cup and saucer, none of which is available. Finally, when they purchase a wooden box, the assistant is unable to wrap it because she has no paper or string.

Yvonne and Suzanne may have listened to a wireless programme called *The Week in Westminster*, in which an MP offered a personal view of events in the House of Commons.[9] This week it was the turn of Sir Herbert Williams, MP for Croydon South, the constituency next to Yvonne's. His wit and devotion to political minutiae had attracted the attention of the BBC and that April he delivered three editions of the programme. In particular, he had fun reporting on a debate about encouraging scientific research, in which Captain Plugge, MP for Chatham, claimed that in future, 'certain developments now taking place will enable us to detach our minds from our bodies for the purpose of business journeys.' Williams imagined that any such detached minds might make a mistake on their journey home and end up in the wrong bodies; at the thought of which, he observed, 'members glanced at each other and considered the possibilities.'[10]

There are always some MPs who, having realised that they are not ministerial material, settle for a career on the backbenches holding others to account. Williams is one of them. He is often described as the 'Tory watchdog,' his mission in politics being, as he sees it, to guard Britain day and night and bark at the first sniff of socialism, government bureaucracy or infringements of individual liberty. Today, when a Labour MP asks Sir James Grigg, Secretary of State for War, the leading question, 'how many native [sic] commissioned officers are there in the Armed Forces of the Crown?' and Sir James regrets that he does not have this information to hand, Sir Herbert waspishly ridicules the questioner, asking, 'Is a Welshman in a Welsh regiment to be regarded as a native?'[11]He also wants to know whether despatches from the battle at Montecassino have been deliberately held back to conceal 'blunders,'[12]argues against the imposition of purchase tax on wooden-soled footwear[13]and, in a debate about repeated incidences of boys absconding from Rochester Borstal, suggests more should be made of the boys' abilities as they appeared to be more intelligent than their guards.[14]

May 1944, Scotland. It's three days before the District Commissioner is due to arrive in Stirling to inspect rescue-service personnel and meet senior Civil Defence staff,[15] and Clem is annoyed again. One of his Home Guard battalions has absented itself from a training session.

> 'Captain Younger ... states that arrangements were made with ... 3 Stirling Battalion for a lecture to be given at Drill Hall, Denny, 1930 hrs 3 May, on the subject of rescue work, to the Denny Platoon. The instructor arrived at 1850 and members of the Platoon duly appeared. Before 1930, however, a senior officer arrived and marched the Home Guard off to range practice. I have asked 3 Stirling for a report.'[16]

Major John Paterson, Captain Adjutant at the Drill Hall, Denny, duly replies that a sergeant had sent some of the platoon off to the shooting ranges. He will ensure this does not happen again. From other documents it seems that the Home Guard enjoyed the shooting ranges much more than any other form of training.

It's nearly time for what Yvonne calls the 'boating party'. On Monday May 15th, Churchill, King George VI, the Chiefs of Staff, members of the War Cabinet and various military personnel from the US and

Britain gather at St Paul's School in Barnes, West London, currently in use as General Montgomery's London HQ. Here, General Eisenhower, Supreme Allied Commander in Europe, announces that, providing the weather is favourable Operation Overlord will begin in three weeks' time with the D-Day landings. In a couple of days troops will move to secure holding camps near the coast for final briefings, ready to embark for France in the first week of June.

It is absolutely crucial that the invasion succeeds. If it fails, the consequences for the Allies will be disastrous: British morale will suffer a huge blow, Churchill and his government will almost certainly be thrown out of office and with them all organised resistance to the Nazis. The Americans will abandon Europe. Stalin will agree terms with Hitler, as he did in 1939. The war, the country and the Empire will be lost.

Everyone knows the attack is imminent. Purley people are apprehensive and excited, swithering between being fervently tight-lipped—as posters constantly remind them, 'Careless talk costs lives'—and an urge to soothe their anxiety by speculation. Aircraft roar overhead; lorries, tanks and trucks rattle along the Brighton Road. Yvonne feels she is closer to the war than Clem. However, his priority seems to be having his socks repaired.

Tuesday, 16th May, 10.30 pm.

My dearest Mr S.,

Huh. So, you've decided to continue to recognise my existence after all, eh? Just to prove what a nice, forgiving disposition I have, here is a reply after only one day's interval, but let me warn you that if I have to wait another 20 days for an enquiry as to my welfare, the next news you get of me will be through my solicitors.

Turning to more mundane matters, and the subject that seems to be your main preoccupation—SOCKS—why these abject apologies for raising the question? It seems to me to be just about the last wifely function left for me to fulfil. In fact, I would say that having someone to darn one's socks is the only logical reason for anyone in the army to consider getting married for (can you sort that one out?) My only complaint is that you <u>will</u> hoard them until the whole collection are in tatters, instead of instituting a sort of fortnightly shuttle service which would be far less strain on my nervous system. Better let me have your new coupons too, when you get them, and I will carry on with the one purl, one plain mixture. Will the day ever come when I can knit in anything else but navy or khaki?

Oh, these bills. I don't think I can possibly be living within my allowance, but I'm damned if I know what else to cut down. However, all my contemporaries appear to be in the same boat. I don't think the new increases will make much difference to you or me. They seem to work out at a couple of shillings a week generally. Rupert had a rise on completing three year's service, to wit, 3d a day! I call it an insult to a qualified man.

Suzanne and I had a session with an old clothes woman last week. I parted with three evening dresses for 15/-. Sick transit and all that. (Don't write back and correct my spelling). 'Don't you worry, dear,' she said, ' the war will soon be over and you'll be dancing again'. I felt she was cheap at the price.

Oliver is all agog waiting for the chocolate. He studied your yesterday's letter very thoroughly and then said, "What for, he hasn't sent me a kiss this time!" So, you see you've started something. Not much chance of him forgetting you. He still tells all and sundry how you pretended to be a dragon at his birthday party[17], how you can lift him up to the ceiling and that you have to stay in Scotland to fight the Germans. There is also a daily joke at the breakfast table about "Mr Porridge" and "Mr Bacon" meeting inside his tummy, which apparently you instigated.

Thanks for the return of the photos. Perhaps your mother would like the one of you with him.

I'll send them on and ask her to tea. We've had a perfect month of fine weather without, I should say, a drop of rain, but the temperature has suddenly dropped right back to winter, and I've had to start coal fires again. If we don't get rain very soon it will be a disastrous year for fruit and vegetables. I have started to water the raspberries and blackcurrants surreptitiously. The earth is like iron, and even the weeds are wilting.

The new baby is behaving with decorum. In fact, I forget at times we have one in the house. He has to be woken up for meals and already weighs over 11 lbs. Strictly entre nous, I still think he isn't a patch on our little maggot, but maybe I'm biased. Oliver is very impatient for him to walk and wants to know why he is always so tired. Rupert "walked out" again on Saturday evening and spent Sunday here, arriving back in Manchester at 5 am on Monday. I pity his last patient that day.

I borrowed Scrupe on Sunday morning to escort me next door to celebrate Gordon Lindsay [family doctor]'s 50th birthday. Unaccustomed as I am to public drinking, I felt delightfully vague after two gins and came back to finish the cooking of the meal of the week at 2 pm. Which reminds me that the reason for my writing being more peculiar than ever is that I sliced the top off one finger while carving the fibrous tissue known as the week's joint. If it goes on like this I shall become a vegetarian by choice. I'd rather spend 1/6d on a lettuce than on something that even the cat can't masticate.

The second front makes me feel awfully lugubrious, when I have time to consider it. Scrupe cheered me up a bit by saying that it can't possibly fail and that all the High Ups are equally confident. How the Jerries must long for it to begin.

No more news, except that I've contrived to get the prints framed at last, and the wireless is back with what almost amounts to a new inside. £2 to pay, but the reception is now so good it's almost worth it.

Connubial caresses and marital meditations. Or, if you prefer it, lots of love,

Y.

P.S. Kindly re-read page 1.

This letter reveals more of the everyday difficulties of wartime: Clem posting his socks to Yvonne for mending, her need for coupons to buy the wool; her trying to manage bills on an army wage and her brother's pitiful pay rise. It's interesting too, that she felt 'lugubrious' about the coming invasion and that her brother tried to cheer her up about it.

Still, her 'rebuke' produced a response from Clem and nine days later she writes to him again.

Thursday, 25th May 1944, 9.30pm.

Dear darling,

Migawd. Whatever's come over you? Two letters in five days and without waiting for a reply in between. Bloody nuisance, as it practically blackmails me into writing tonight. And there I am with three hours of ironing piled up in the kitchen. And I haven't mentally composed my weekly homily yet, not having any socks or winter woollies to prattle about happily page after page.

This sudden onslaught of calligraphic diarrhoea is supposed, I imagine, to get me into an equable frame of mind to tackle the fragrant parcel, which you describe with such wealth of detail. "Bung a couple of kisses at the bottom of the last page," I can hear you say, "and the old girl will send 'em back in a couple of days". You poor sap, I can read you like a book in Basic English.

So, my first wifely duty is to look after your suits, eh? Huh. Well, I suppose that's just about all I am fit for, seeing as how you have given the best years of your wife to the army. I may say that, having contracted the habit of popping [selling] my old clothes, I shall probably start on yours one day soon when I need a couple of bob to tide me over until Saturday.

Mamma treated Oliver and me to a day at the Zoo on Monday and I must say I have never enjoyed the place more, although I must have been half a dozen times as a kid. Rows of empty cages and never a keeper in sight, but quite enough for Oliver to take in. He had rides on everything going, the camel, donkey and in the llama and pony traps. Liked the gazelles best of all, and now wants one in the garden. Calls them Bambis, of course.

Apart from that, our other sole outing has been to a birthday party in South Croydon, a large one with fifteen kids and ten mothers. Oliver is definitely not sociable (at any rate not yet). He wouldn't play oranges and lemons and wanted to sit on the swing by himself all the afternoon. Looks like becoming a bookworm. He sits for ages studying the pictures and even tries to sneak one on the table at meal times. Needless to say, this doesn't meet with my approval. One like that in the family is quite enough! He's also started a craze for cutting out, and the dining room generally resembles a paper chase. I spend ages collecting the bits, which are alike to me, and then it's 'Oh Mummie, you've taken away my rabbit, horse, parrot, etc. which I've cut out specially for keeping'.

While I think of it, he wants me to ask you how you keep up your pyjama trousers, as his always slip down unless he holds them all the time. Must be something to do with his fat stomach, I think.

Have been getting around to some of your records lately. There are some surprises. Do you know that the first two records of Tchaikovsky's Violin Concerto are missing from the album, and the one labelled Beethoven Concerto No 4 contains Symphony No 5? Odd. Oliver adores "Round the Marble Arch" and Rimsky-Korsakov's "Flight of the Bumble Bee."

Conversation at tea table with the Vicar of St James's. Heavy going but we want him for the baby's christening.

Vicar (to Jennie): How about coming to my Sunday school?

Jennie (graciously): I hate Sunday schools.

(Embarrassed pause)

Vicar (turning to Oliver): How about you?

Oliver (firmly): I would rather go to the zoo!

Heigh ho, my darling. Shall I be seeing you before the beech leaves fall, or the September telephone bill comes in?

Love and so forth,

Y.

Clem's record collection consists of 78 rpm shellac discs, each the size of a dinner plate. These would have rotated on the gramophone turntable so fast that only about ten minutes of music could be contained on one side, so a concerto or symphony had to be spread across multiple discs, and playing it all the way through required the listener to get up every few minutes and turn over or replace the disc. If played frequently, the discs wore out. As a listening experience it left something to be desired.

Meanwhile in Scotland, the owner of the record collection is busy. The colonel commanding the Perthshire Sub-District has issued a warning that, to divert the Allies' attention from the invasion, an attack may be launched on the Rosyth Dockyard. Helpfully, the document warns that news of the attack may either come late in the evening when members of the Home Guard are asleep in their beds, or during the daytime when they will be at work. Clem notes the key areas to be defended and especially the instruction that reconnaissance cars are to patrol the dockyard, ready at a moment's notice to 'shoot up the enemy who may break in'.[18]

However, this order raises a question. If members of the Home Guard who work in the dockyard are to be ready at a moment's notice, should they bring their weapons and uniforms with them every day when they come to work? Yes, says the colonel, what a good idea. The men can carry everything they need in bags, like schoolboys with P.E. kits. Then, after a pause, the order is countermanded. Good heavens! Weapons can't be left 'lying about' in the yard while men are working on the ships! Another instruction follows: The men must wear their uniforms to work and back again, and keep their weapons beside them at all times.[19] Clear? Let's hope the best brains in the British Army are working on D-Day.

May becomes June and the Whitsun weekend weather is glorious. At Foxley Lodge, beneath the trees at the edge of The Wood, Yvonne relaxes in a deckchair. She keeps half an eye on Jennie and Oliver, who are doing something mysterious with a Pinocchio doll which Rupert sewed together for her from odd bits of fabric. Jennie is tying it to a tree with a cord that looks suspiciously like the one belonging to Clem's old dressing gown while Oliver waves a stick which Jennie calls a 'Tommy hawk'. Yvonne decides not to intervene.

She folds the newspaper. It's too hot to concentrate on war news. The wireless said crowds are expected at Lords for the cricket and Ascot for the horse-racing, so perhaps everyone is taking the opportunity to enjoy themselves before the invasion and the inevitable retaliatory attacks which will follow. From a wicker basket on the ground beside her, she takes out one of Clem's socks and starts darning, one ear alert all the while to the children.

Suzanne crosses the lawn carrying the baby and sits beside her. Just as she is about to speak, a large formation of planes appears in the sky, heading south. The baby, dozily perched on his mother's lap, looks up to see where this terrific noise is coming from and, once they have gone by, stares goggle-eyed at his mother's wrist, at a bracelet glinting in the dappled sunlight. Yvonne notices it too. That's her charm bracelet, she thinks, worn for luck. A glance is exchanged between the women, but nothing is said.

It won't be long now before tens of thousands of young men land on the beaches of Normandy and Yvonne will have far greater concerns than sorting out a record collection or tying pyjama trousers. Hitler has something special lined up for Purley.

Chapter 2
June 12th to July 10th 1944

'I am ready to foam at the mouth if I read another article stating that the people in the South are proud to be in the front line again.'

June 12th 1944: Monday, nearly a week after D-Day.

Along a 60-mile stretch of French coast, Allied ships are unloading tanks, troops, guns and other supplies. At around 11 o'clock on one beach, a group of soldiers stops work to watch a barge arrive on the sands. A familiar figure disembarks. Instantly recognisable by his portly build and round-cheeked face, he's wearing a Trinity House peaked cap, double-breasted coat and well-pressed trousers. He salutes them with his signature V-sign. Winston has landed.

General Montgomery, equally recognisable in his flying jacket and beret, arrives in a jeep. A cameraman films Churchill climbing aboard and lighting a cigar while cheering soldiers surround the two leaders. They drive away and at Monty's gypsy-cabin HQ, over lunch, Churchill is briefed on the current situation before visiting Courseulles-sur-Mer, a town liberated a few days earlier and earmarked as a depot for Canadian forces. More cheering soldiers. Churchill does not see or, if he does, chooses to ignore, a crude Nazi propaganda poster stuck to a wall depicting him as a scowling, cigar-smoking octopus with bloodied and severed tentacles.

The destroyer that brought Churchill now conveys him along the French coast. Keen to play his part in the hostilities, he asks the commander to fire on German positions inland, hoping to provoke a response. To his great regret, the salvo is ignored. Finally, as the sun sets, he and his party sail back across the Channel to Portsmouth.[20]

Next day, the Germans respond. At daybreak, two men from the Royal Observer Corps scanning the skies from a Martello Tower near Dymchurch in Kent spot a small, strange aircraft flying towards them. It can't be a plane because it's far too small for a pilot to fit inside. It looks like a metal tube with stubby wings and flames spurting out of its back end. And it makes a very loud, stuttering noise like an old car going uphill.[21]

The observers have been warned to look out for something like this and immediately identify it. Mr Woodland, who bears a slight resemblance to Captain Mainwairing of *Dad's Army,* passes to his control room in Maidstone the codeword, 'Diver!'[22] Sirens sound and Fighter Command is informed, but within a few minutes Diver's engine has cut out. It glides down on to open ground in Gravesend and explodes.[23]

More Divers follow. Nine are spotted over Kent, Surrey and Sussex, one of which blows out the glass in a couple of greenhouses, killing several chickens. Another flies over Croydon, where a group of policemen cheer, thinking it is an enemy plane on fire. Yet another reaches Bethnal Green in East London, where it detonates on a railway bridge. Six people are killed, 30 injured, 200 made homeless.

The Chiefs of Staff meet, followed by the War Cabinet. For some time, both committees have known that the Germans have been developing two secret weapons: a pilotless plane and a rocket bomb. Both agree Diver is the former and to their considerable relief seems to be a much less accurate and dangerous missile than they had anticipated. In fact, the Germans seem to have sent over some sort of prototype, presumably to draw the Allies' attention away from military action in France. Air Marshal Roderick Hill reports he is confident there is no need to implement his defence plan because the anti-aircraft guns will shoot down any more of these invaders.

However, two days later, on Thursday June 15th, the situation becomes more serious. Divers appear in larger numbers: 155 arrive over the south coast; 144 travel inland, heading for London. In the dark and cloudy skies, the AA (anti-aircraft) gunners and hastily scrambled fighter pilots can't see them clearly, but nevertheless manage to shoot down 21.[24] Some 73 reach the London area, dropping and exploding on a range of sites from St Pancras to Sutton in Surrey, killing 165 people and destroying numerous buildings.

In Croydon the air-raid sirens sound from midnight through to midday on Friday. A gunner aims at a Diver but misses, the shell explodes near Croydon Airport and kills both a fire watcher and an air-raid warden. Eight more Divers land in Croydon, one close to the Royal Oak pub on the Brighton Road, only ten minutes from Foxley Lodge. Elderly boot repairer Tom Skilton, his wife Alice and their 19-year-old neighbour, Emma Anderson, lose their lives. The windows of a passing bus are shattered by the blast and passengers are cut by flying glass; eight houses are wrecked and a further five seriously damaged. An air-raid warden is later quoted as saying, "This was something we definitely hadn't bargained for... I don't mind admitting that for a moment my knees shook and I was scared stiff... I have forgotten all about our invasion of France."[25]

For a population now wearily accustomed to bombs being dropped at night from piloted planes, Diver is something completely different: it's unpredictable, inhuman and sinister. What exactly is it? How does it work? And what is its purpose?

Hitler believes Germany's defeat in the First World War was because its people lost the will to continue fighting and is determined this won't happen again. The Allies are heavily bombing German towns and cities: he needs to demonstrate that he can protect his people and avenge their losses, that he is fighting back. This will secure their loyalty and boost their morale.

But how? Hitler has taken note that no less a person than the abdicated King Edward VIII, now the Duke of Windsor, has told him the best way to subjugate the British is to drop bombs on them.[26] London, the centre of the British Empire and its seat of government, must be the target and if it can be obliterated, the war will be won. After all, the Führer believes that democratic governments are weak because they are obliged to respond to their citizens' demands. So, if he can rain down bombs on the capital, the British population will protest, rise up and overthrow Churchill's government, allowing him to march in and install the Duke as his puppet king. This scenario appeals greatly to his megalomaniac fantasies.

But there's a snag. Since 1941 the RAF has controlled the airspace over Britain and the Luftwaffe has been unable to launch air raids on anything like the same scale as the 1940 Blitz. What Hitler needs is a way to deliver bombs without jeopardising his planes and crews. So he authorises the Wehrmacht, the German Army, to develop the Diver or, as it is known in Germany, Vergeltungswaffe Eins, 'Revenge Weapon 1' or 'V1'; and the Luftwaffe to develop a rocket bomb, or V2. The purpose of both weapons isn't military. It is to create terror by causing massive destruction, killing civilians indiscriminately and collapsing British morale.

The V1 is a pilotless plane, the world's first unguided missile. It is small, jet-propelled and controlled by an automatic pilot, filled with high explosive and enough fuel to reach London. When it lands, it detonates outwards creating an immense surface blast that can be felt miles away, leaving only a shallow crater. Without a crew and with only one journey to make, it is lightweight and quick to produce. Cheap too: its price is only about 2% of the price of a twin-engined bomber. There are no labour costs either because it is manufactured on a production line using expendable slaves—prisoners whose labour is incidental to their being worked to death in the most appalling conditions in an underground factory in central Germany. From here, each V1 is delivered at night by rail to a field depot in France and taken to its launch site, most of which are in the Pas de Calais, to be fired from a simple ramp towards London. It takes about 20 minutes to arrive.

Early in the morning of Friday June 16th, following the overnight salvo, the Chiefs of Staff meet. They note that Divers are coming in greater numbers and are more dangerous than had at first been assumed. What can be done? At noon, the War Cabinet meets: Churchill, Attlee, Eden, Bevin and Morrison with Bracken, Beaverbrook, the neatly trimmed Jan Smuts from South Africa and Sir Hari Singh, the last ruling Maharajah of Jammu and Kashmir, currently serving a three-month stint as representative from British Imperial India. It's a mix of public schools, gentlemen's clubs, military college and the hard knocks of poverty and trade unionism. They are, of course, all men. Watch chains glint on waistcoats, their suits carry lapels as wide as V-signs; ties except for Winston's polka-dot bow, are sober. Tobacco smoke and a tang of shoe polish thicken the air. They review the situation and advice from the Chiefs. It's clear now that London is the target not, as might have been anticipated, Allied forces in France or the Channel ports, and it is also uncomfortably obvious that it won't be possible to stop all of them from getting through.

Churchill authorises implementation of defensive measures. First, a belt of artillery will be assembled across the North Downs to shoot down the missiles. Fighter planes are given an operational area covering the skies from the Channel to the first 20 miles or so inland from the

Kent and Sussex coast. It will be some time before ground troops in France will be able to reach and destroy the launch sites and almost impossible for bombers to hit them from the air as they are hidden deep in woodland. However, Churchill agrees to ask Eisenhower to allow any planes that can be spared from Normandy to attack supply lines in northern France.

There is a further line of defence, one which takes advantage of the V1 being pilotless. The Germans will be desperate to know the accuracy of their aim, where the bombs are landing and how much damage they cause. The Cabinet agrees to starve them of any such information. Rules are quickly agreed with newspaper editors, newsreels and the BBC. Reports will be restricted to mentioning only that 'pilotless planes' are falling in 'Southern England.' The first example of this is at lunchtime, when the BBC's news bulletin announces as its third item that 'the enemy has started using pilotless planes against this country'.[27]

The Cabinet also discusses what this 'bomb with wings' should be called, and agrees that for official purposes 'flying bomb,' or 'Fly' will be used. 'Diver' is largely abandoned. By now other names are already circulating, such as 'buzz bomb' and 'farting fanny' after the noise it makes. 'Pilotless plane' and Churchill's favourite, 'robot' also gain currency, the latter being less popular perhaps because it implies the missile is autonomous. However, the origin of the name by which it becomes most widely known is described in the *Croydon Times* thus: 'Fighter Pilots have christened the Maniac Nazis' latest terror weapon the "Doodle Bug."'[28] Associating the terror weapon with a small American insect best known for blowing holes out of its bum makes it seem ridiculous and less frightening. The name is officially encouraged.

After the Cabinet meeting, Minister of Home Security Herbert Morrison reports to the House of Commons. A Londoner and long-serving Labour politician, he delivers his statement, stressing the need to avoid giving 'the enemy any information which would help him... by telling him where his missiles have landed,' and warning that more 'pilotless aircraft' will follow. In the meantime, people must carry on 'as normal' while not 'exposing themselves unnecessarily to danger by remaining in the streets out of curiosity, instead of taking the nearest cover while the guns are firing.'[29] Public confirmation of what is happening encourages Yvonne to send Clem her own account.

Friday June 16th, Purley.

My dear darling,

For the past 24 hours we have had our first experience of the pilotless planes, and not very nice it's been. They came over at intervals from midnight until half past nine this morning, and since then we have had five separate alerts, which has meant that most of the time was spent popping in and out of the shelter.

Of course they arrived for lunch and tea, but I did manage to get round the shops hurriedly on the bike during a lull. There's one now, but we are all prepared for the night in the shelter. The kids can get in, that is, and Suzanne and I will sleep on the floor. We had the fire going today and have everything aired.

They sound just like ordinary planes to me, but just when they are overhead (or rather, so it seems) the engine stops and there's a horrible wait of seconds before the crash comes.

The barrage was going great guns last night, but I don't see the point of hitting them or trying to bring them down, they'll make a mess anyway, won't they?

I have got the wind up a bit[30] and feel rather depressed at having to face this sort of thing all over again in a new form, but it's probably first night nerves and we shall get used to it in the long run. Seeing the casualties being taken in at the hospital this morning was a pity, but it couldn't be helped. The district round the Royal Oak got it worse, some houses in the Brighton Road too. You feel so bloody helpless, more than ever.

You haven't written for such a long time. I don't really know if you ever give us a thought.

Y.

In the past 24 hours, nearly 50 bombs have fallen in boroughs south of Central London. Official guidance to wives writing to their servicemen husbands recommended they should make light of their difficulties so as not to cause their man anxiety or distract him from his duties. Yvonne does try; she gives him the facts and puts on a brave face, but this weapon, which has appeared so suddenly and is so unpredictable, is terrifying. She is too honest, too expressive and too close to Clem to pretend otherwise. The V1s aren't being stopped by the guns nor is there any hint of a more effective defence. She and Suzanne have two young children and a new baby to protect.

Yvonne wakes from a nightmare. She saw a pram rolling downhill, going faster and faster with no means of stopping. For several minutes she lies on a camp bed in the shelter, calming her racing heart and rapid breathing. It's early morning. She is listening with razor-sharp ears, alert for sirens, throaty engines and explosions, but for the moment all she hears is birdsong and the quiet breaths of the sleeping others in the shelter. The fear is exhausting though, fear of the doodlebugs, fear of what might become of you or God help you, your child; let alone the fear of losing your nerve.

Everything I will do today, she thinks, shopping, cooking, cleaning, must be done quickly and in a state of suppressed anxiety. It simply seems safer to stay indoors and look after yourself. Later that day, in the queue outside the greengrocer's, she notices everyone talking about the 'doodlebugs', how many have landed and where: the casualties, the wreckage, what neighbours have told them. Even though some of the women are already grey with sleeplessness they try to sound brave and cheerful. After all, it could be worse. There's a war on. Mustn't grumble. Yvonne feels no obligation to keep everyone else's spirits up. In fact, she wishes someone would admit to being absolutely terrified of the things. But no one does.

In her letter, Yvonne described the sound of a doodlebug as being like that of an ordinary plane, which is unusual because most observers compared it to an old car or a motorbike, but she does mention something that everyone commented on: the eerie silence just before it dropped; a silence that told you that someone, somewhere was about to become a victim.

At first, there is no explanation for the silence. Everyone assumes it is because the doodlebug has run out of fuel and, even after the real reason is discovered, this isn't contradicted because it conceals the fact that the flying bomb is actually a very clever piece of design. German engineers have calculated from test flights the number of revolutions the bomb's small propeller needs to make for it to reach central London. Once this number has been achieved, two explosive bolts are fired, lifting its tail and tilting it into a steep dive. Then, because the hammering from the vanes of its pulse jet engine has weakened the shutters, the engine cuts out and the doodlebug glides silently to the ground.[31]

The news blackout prompts the Wehrmacht into action. This evening, a German military intelligence officer sends a secret message to one of his spies in North London. 'It is of the utmost importance to inform us of the effects of the bombardments,' he writes, and instructs the agent to get a copy of a specific map of London, rule it with a squared grid, locate the places where the flying bombs have landed and send him the results.[32]

Unfortunately for him, all German spies in Britain have been either executed or turned into double agents by the Secret Services. This one, codenamed 'Garbo', is participating in a secret operation run by John Masterman, a name evocative of Victorian adventure novels, in which entirely false information is being sent to his German handler. Garbo's codename is deliciously ironic, Greta Garbo was a film star famous for saying that she wanted 'to be alone', but this Garbo and his handler, Tomás (Tommy) Harris have dreamt up a network of 26 entirely fictitious sub-agents, each one supplying the Germans with fake information.

Garbo has been taking part in a major deception called Fortitude South. Its purpose is to convince Hitler that the D-Day landings are a feint with the real invasion coming later at Calais. The plan has worked so effectively that Hitler is still holding troops there instead of sending them as reinforcements to Normandy. However, it has also meant that the agents must continue to invent and report fake information for much longer than they had anticipated. Masterman and his team, initially elated at their success, are by now feeling 'tired and jaded.'[33]

But what to do? Garbo must answer the request from his German contact or his credibility, and with it that of Fortitude South's, will start to look suspect; but if he sends accurate information, the Germans will refine the V1s' aim.

So Garbo stalls. He sends an innocuous reply also designed to extract useful information. 'I am very tired,' his message sighs. 'I have been unable to sleep because of the air-raid alerts "all last night" in London.' He asks if V1s will continue to be fired every night. Should he move away from the capital? He ends his message with the reassurance that an 'attack' on Calais from Dover and Folkestone is imminent.[34]

Sunday June 18th: just before 11:20 am, a man standing on Westminster Bridge watches in alarm as a V1 appears in the sky above Waterloo Station and heads across the river. His first thought is that it is going to hit the Houses of Parliament but, to his relief, it passes over them. A couple of second later the engine stops and it falls out of sight.

It lands in Birdcage Walk, on the compound belonging to the Army's elite Guards' Division, hitting its chapel. The concrete roof, patched up after earlier bomb damage, collapses entirely. The upper walls cave in. Huge slabs of masonry, timber and glass crash onto the congregation below; worshippers who had one moment been listening to the reading of a Lesson are now lying in the dark, amid dust, debris and the dead.

It takes two days for everyone to be dug out, the rubble is ten feet deep in places. Members of the rescue squads suffer traumatic after-effects for the rest of their lives from having excavated body parts. Some 121 people, both civilian and military, are dead, and 141 are seriously injured, some of them members of Australian, Free French and American forces. Of the 56 civilian deaths, the majority are women; 18 are over 60 years old and ten are the wives or daughters of commissioned officers. Two are titled: Lady Gwendolen Lumley-Smith, the wife of a major and daughter of a late 19th-century commandant of Cairo City Police; and Lady Evelyn Gordon-Lennox, widow of Major The Lord Bernard Charles Gordon-Lennox and daughter of Baron Loch of Drylaw, a man who had enjoyed a varied and adventurous career on behalf of the British Empire in China, Australia and South Africa.

Guards' Chapel is not the only building hit today. Across London, a further 380 civilian lives are lost to V1s: 77 in Wandsworth, 24 in Battersea and 19 in Hackney. In Winchelsey Rise in Croydon, Police Inspector William Holloway squeezes into a collapsed air-raid shelter to rescue a mother and her baby. They are safely brought out but her badly injured three-year-old daughter remains trapped. Realising she is not going to survive, and even though he is aware that the roof above them may collapse at any minute, Holloway stays with the little girl, comforting her until she dies. For this he is awarded the British Empire Medal. The mother is unable to salvage anything from the wreck of her house and is left with her baby and 'no pram, no nappies, not even a bottle and no home,'[35] although she is later found temporary accommodation and supported by the Women's Voluntary Service.

At 6 pm, the Chiefs of Staff meet in the War Room, a secret bunker in Whitehall, deep underground, where military staff work day and night collating information, updating huge wall maps and formulating future plans. The meeting is called in response to today's attacks, especially the one on Guards' Chapel, and it's an indication of the seriousness with which the V1 attacks are now being taken that Churchill and

Herbert Morrison also attend. This afternoon, military police whisked Churchill's wife to safety in her Kent family home.[36]

Ever since the flying bombs arrived, it's been assumed the Germans will try to improve their aim and it looks like today they have. On the anniversary of the Battle of Waterloo, a flying bomb has struck the heart of the British establishment. Birdcage Walk is only a few minutes' walk from Buckingham Palace, Westminster Abbey, Whitehall and Downing Street, and the gentlemen's clubs of Pall Mall, Piccadilly and Jermyn Street, where politicians, businessmen and members of the secret service privately meet.

The Chiefs, sitting on their wooden chairs in front of the politicians, listen as Morrison reports the statistics for the previous 24 hours' attacks. They promise that by the end of the week AA guns will be ready on the North Downs and that barrage balloons are being rushed from across the country to provide a defensive wall behind them. Fighter pilots are trying to shoot down as many flying bombs as possible, while bombers continue to fly sorties over northern France. They are doing all they can.

But is there anything else that can be done, something... less orthodox?

MI5's Flight Lieutenant Charles Cholmondeley has an idea. He's an eccentric character, very tall, luxuriously moustached and self-effacing. His involvement in covert missions such as Operation Mincemeat has gained him a favourable reputation in secret-service circles. He makes his way to an office in Westminster and calls in to see Assistant Director of Intelligence R.V. Jones. They both know, having read records of V1 test flights previously smuggled out to them, that the flying bombs have a tendency to fall short of their target. They consult a plot of where the flying bombs have landed in the first 24 hours and discover they that are, indeed, falling two or three miles short of what they assume to be the aiming point, Trafalgar Square.

Can this information be used to their advantage? The only accurate piece of information the Germans have is the time at which each V1 is fired. Jones quickly realises that if it is possible to fool them into linking the firing times of bombs that have landed in south London with the landing points of those that fell to the north, there is a chance they will shorten their range. This would give the inner London boroughs, including Mayfair and Westminster, some protection, although it would mean suburbs further south would bear the brunt of the attacks. But these are less densely populated, so the end result would be fewer casualties.

Later that evening, five men meet secretly at 58 St James's Street, deep in the heart of Clubland: Sir Samuel Findlater Stewart, Chairman of the Home Defence Executive; Guy Liddell, in charge of counter-espionage, Cholmondeley, Masterman and Harris. They know it is critical that the secret agents continue reporting to their German handlers. Cholmondeley puts forward his and Jones's plan and after ten minutes Liddell leaves to attend a meeting of the Joint Intelligence Committee.

Here, Liddell asks for guidance as to whether the Jones/Cholmondeley plan should be adopted and what the risks might be should such a deception be uncovered; by this he means uncovered by the enemy, rather than by civilians who would be put in the firing line. An air commodore expresses concern because he has heard that some V1s are equipped with wireless apparatus to transmit data about their course and landing points back to the launch crews. If so, reporting misinformation will wreck the credibility of the double agents. The commodore is correct, some V1s are fitted with wireless equipment and the length of their transmission gives the distance the bomb has travelled. Fortunately for the British, one of the first to do so landed near Tower Bridge, convincing the Germans they were right on target and less attention was paid to wireless data after that.

Liddell reports back to the first group and tonight's message from Garbo praises 'this fantastic reprisal weapon, the creation of German genius... I am certain that you will manage to terrify this very pusillanimous people who never will admit that they are beaten.' He promises to obtain a copy of the map they want him to use and to 'identify and send back the locations of the fall of shot,' before adding, misleadingly, that the area where the bombs have landed is, 'extensive... from Harwich to Portsmouth, circling London to the north and west,' thereby hinting already that some V1s have overshot their target.[37] Thus begins the deception plan. On paper, it seems reasonable. But isn't there something uncomfortable about a secret service deciding to deliberately sacrifice one section of the population to spare another? Are they entitled to make this decision?

This weekend, Churchill, who had been cheered for his presence on the Normandy beaches on Monday, is in a sombre mood, while the opposite can be said of his antagonist. Hitler is thrilled by the success of 'his' revenge weapon. He flies to Northern France to congratulate the generals and, ignoring their concerns that the campaign will provoke more intense Allied bombing raids on Germany, orders an increase in the supply of V1s. Flying bombs will force the Allies to divert their attention from the war in France, he says: they will save the Fatherland.[38]

Monday June 19th: A Pathé cameraman arrives in Fitzrovia's Whitfield Street shortly after a doodlebug has struck, one of many to arrive this day. He films the aftermath. The narrow road is a scene of devastation: bodies are being dug out of huge banks of debris and carried off under blankets on wire stretchers, the bearers teetering and stumbling on scattered broken bricks, wooden planks and shattered glass. Dust is suspended in the air. A young man in a sports jacket and tie stares about him, immobile and dazed, while behind him air-raid wardens and civil defence workers in a human chain pass bricks and wood along the line, clearing the rubble. The front of a building has been destroyed, exposing a mantelpiece on an upper floor, with the family's ornaments still in place.[39]

Among the 31 civilian fatalities here are nine merchant seamen from Turkey and India; an ambulance driver, Shuraj Ali, also from India; Maria Bruno from Sant'Ambrogio di Torino in Italy and her mother-in-law, and Bertha Gleghorn; a woman police officer who had just stepped out of Tottenham Court Road Police Station to set off on her beat.

In the next few days, the AA guns and barrage balloons are finally assembled along the North Downs. Each of the balloons is about 62 feet long and attached by steel cables to winches on static lorries. It is partly filled with hydrogen gas which has to be topped up every day and a permanent ground crew is needed to keep it afloat. However, people in nearby towns are unhappy: they fear the doodlebugs will be caught up in the cables and dragged down to explode on them. Not far from Purley, roofs are damaged when a balloon escapes from its winch and drags its cable across a row of houses, tearing off roof tiles. As it turns out, the barrage is of limited use because the spaces between the cables is often wide enough for the doodlebugs to sail between them.

On Wednesday June 21st, a week and a day after the first doodlebugs arrived, Yvonne writes again to Clem. Life at Foxley Lodge seems a little calmer... or she is putting a brave face on it.

Dear darling,

Thanks for the letter, which seems to have done me a lot of good. Matter of fact, I've been feeling a bit ashamed of my last effort to you, but it was written after a sleepless night and a chaotic day, and it would have been different if you had been here. However, I've slept soundly for two nights, in my own bed with Oliver beside me, only waking for the noisier boomps. Oliver sleeps like a log, I don't think even the house falling down would disturb him.

I've given over the shelter to Suzanne and Jennie, the baby sleeps under the stairs in the gas cupboard. It was quite hopeless all mucking in together. We tried it for two nights but then came to the conclusion that we would be better all round in separate families. You see, Jennie always wakes at every siren (and we get plenty) and she cried out and woke Oliver and the baby, who took ages (the baby that is) to be pacified. It seems to me that the main thing is to stick with your children, after all even shelters aren't 100%. Witness the house in Green Lane which was hit this week. Two little boys downstairs in shelter were killed, parents in bed upstairs only slightly injured.

Actually, we are getting quite blasé about the damn things, and don't bother to go into the shelter at daytime unless they seem to be heading this way. After all, if you can see them passing along, not overhead, you do at least know that they can't turn and chase you and that you've "had it". I've only actually seen three of them, but they are coming over at intervals nearly all the time.

The sirens are just silly. Quite often you hear something drop just after the All Clear, and there are so many of them that you get quite bewildered as to whether it is the Alert or Raiders Passed you are waiting for. They seem to have stopped the barrage, thank God. It wasn't the slightest use and only made a helluva noise for nothing.

One was shot down near Mother's in Chelsea and chose to drop on a hospital. So it seems that unless they can be caught over the sea or open country they are better left alone. I feel, like you, that it won't be long before we shall get the hang of eliminating them, but it's quite true that the newspapers make light of the damage and casualties. Personally I am ready to foam at the mouth if I read another article stating that the people in the South are proud to be in the front line again.

Jennie, by the way, is going back to Manchester with Rupert on Sunday to stay with the family of one of the officers on his station. She is just at the wrong age for this sort of excitement and Suzanne can't really cope with her and the baby. Rupert is coming down on Saturday to collect her. It will be a good thing in more than one way, as she has developed a horrible jealousy complex over the baby and has been behaving very badly for some weeks now, rude and disobedient in the daytime and very naughty when put to bed, shrieking for mother especially when Suzanne goes to look at the baby, etc. I won't bore you with all the scenes we've had. She has been the only one for too long, poor kid. It isn't anything to do with me, but unfortunately she takes it out on Oliver sometimes and then I have to step in with the firm hand.

Oliver doesn't seem to be affected by the raids except that he talks of sirens, big bangs and shooting Germans more than usual. He takes the first two items quite naturally and looks on the shelter as some sort of game. He's not going to be bottom of the form. Already he can pick out all the letters on his bricks except K and Q, and when he learns to write W he will be able to sign his surname! He can copy any letter after he has watched me draw it two or three times, and learns verses and stories by heart very quickly. But, of course, he won't do a thing when I want to show him off!

Haven't told you half the ordinary news, that will have to keep for another letter. We feel very much in the war now, what with what goes down the main roads all day and over our heads, towards the coast I mean, in the early hours of the morning. The news seems to go from good to better, I shall soon believe that there may be an end to the war one day. Not so optimistic as you though. Would you take a bet on it finishing this year?

Love, darling,

Y.

At the best of times, a new baby is a challenge to its siblings, and Jennie has had to adapt to her little brother's arrival while the adults around her are coping with flying bombs. Suzanne's decision to send her away seems to have been prompted as much by her daughter's behaviour as the need for her safety. In later life, Jennie remembered being unhappy in Manchester because she disliked the family she was boarding with and, with her father working all day, she spent most of the time wandering around the RAF camp, bored and lonely, wondering why she had been sent there.

And if leaving a two-and-a-half-month old baby in a 'gas cupboard' under the stairs overnight seems odd, Suzanne is an adherent to the doctrines of popular childhood expert Dr Truby King, who thought it best if babies were kept away from their mothers except at strictly regulated feeding times because it was character-forming. Besides, the gas cupboard was about the safest place for the baby because if a bomb struck, 'only' the stairs and the roof would collapse on him, rather than a whole room of furniture complete with floor and ceiling.

Yvonne's comments about the unreliability of the air-raid sirens are typical. The Cabinet has discussed whether it is necessary for the alarm to be sounded every time a flying bomb appears, especially as they tend to be fired one by one, presumably in order to cause maximum disruption. They agree that the alert will be sounded only once at night and local warnings will be given at places like factories so work isn't constantly interrupted—remember the strombos horns and bugles made permissible in Scotland. Churchill soon tells a Civil Defence meeting it isn't necessary to sound the alert if only one flying bomb is sighted, a decision which turns out to be controversial, as we shall see.

The reason Yvonne notices that the barrage has 'stopped' is because the AA guns that were stationed near Purley have been taken to the North Downs. She also mentions a bomb that fell on a 'hospital in Chelsea'. This is one that landed four days earlier at St Mary Abbott's Hospital. However, the incident at Green Lane in Purley is more mysterious. No record fits her description of the death of two boys in a shelter, but three days previously in Thornton Heath, north of Croydon, three teenage boys and their parents were killed in similar circumstances, so perhaps Yvonne has picked up a garbled version of this incident.

If she did, it is hardly surprising. With a total news blackout, it's impossible for the public to know what is going on other than what they can see for themselves. The newspapers mention only that bombs are landing in open countryside or on empty buildings with 'some damage'. Only the occasional fatality or 'slight' and morally reprehensible casualties are reported. For example, on June 21st, *The*

Times reports that 'About a dozen people, including a doctor and his wife, are known to have been killed when [a flying bomb] demolished a property in a road early yesterday... One flying bomb, caught by a night fighter, hit a house. No one was killed... A number of people were killed and others were injured when a bomb blew off part of the roof of a Baptist church and wrecked a number of houses,' [40] and so on. However, the papers devote much space to praising the fighter pilots who, in a reprise of their heroism in the Battle of Britain, are apparently despatching the flying bombs into the English Channel in huge numbers.

It's all good, morale-lifting propaganda, but it creates a perception in 'Southern England' that the authorities are ignoring and trivialising their predicament. Some residents begin to wonder whether the real reason for the lack of proper information is because the government is covering up a huge disaster. After all, the Allies have the most powerful air force in the world, so why can't the doodlebugs be stopped?

There are several reasons, which of course can't be made public, for this. First, owing to a factory strike earlier in the year, the RAF doesn't have enough of its fastest planes, the Tempests. Second, it is asking a lot of a pilot to spot an object with a 16-ft wingspan travelling at high speed on a clear day, let alone in thick cloud, and dangerous for him to be near it when it detonates 2,000lbs of high explosive. Third, clouds frustrate the gunners, who want to avoid hitting a fighter plane by mistake but, if they hold their fire, can find themselves impotently watching a doodlebug sail by overhead. Lastly, the current demarcation of areas between guns and planes is causing confusion, as writer H.E. Bates puts it, it's like 'two or three boxing matches in a crowded railway carriage.'[41]

As Hiram Johnson famously said, 'The first casualty, when war comes, is truth.' Garbo's messages to his handlers circumvent saying anything useful to them. For example, on June 22nd he writes that there is no point passing information about flying-bomb landing points until their technicians have found a way to make the V1s fly faster so they can evade fighter planes, although he reports that bombs have fallen on various central London landmarks, such as Hyde Park, Green Park, Goodge Street, St Pancras and the Guards' Chapel and which were likely to have been reported to them already by neutral observers. He gives no details. As for the effect on civilian morale, Garbo says 'the device is now being ridiculed' and the public is now unafraid of it.

Deception breeds deception. Garbo is sending his garbled messages, the German news is full of the 'success' of the wonder weapon and the British news blackout prevents both populations from learning the truth. Instead, in the butchers' and bus queues of Britain, wild and exaggerated stories about death and destruction circulate by word of mouth.[42]

The newspapers resort to quirky tales. A woman is rescued from a collapsed house because two wardrobes topple over and lock together, forming a shelter over her head.[43] On hearing the alert siren, another is dragged by the local fishmonger into his fridge for safety.[44] A Croydon woman, caught outdoors with her baby as a doodlebug passes over, hides in a shelter, rigid with fear, and loses all track of time.[45] A tailor, whose shop loses its windows for the third time, puts up a notice saying, 'We are now open day and night.'[46] Sgt Barefoot, an American soldier, survives under a pile of rubble for 85 hours before being dug out,[47] and so on.

In one bizarre episode, Croydon bricklayer Albert Johnson claims to be blessed with mystical powers enabling him to predict where the doodlebugs will land. One evening, he is overheard shouting he will 'lay six to four' that one is going to drop in a particular place. His neighbour, John Henry Pook, reprimands him in less than polite terms, saying he is scaring people and frightening women and children. Johnson lands a punch on him. A policeman is summoned and Johnson arrested, 'half-drunk'. In court, he admits he should not have mentioned his special powers, but claims to have hit Pook under 'extreme provocation' because Pook had called him 'yellow' and another 'uncomplimentary name'. 'Anyone who says that to me I'll choke,' Johnson tells the court. He is fined 20s.[48]

In a speech in the House of Commons, Herbert Morrison responds to critics of the government's news blackout by reminding MPs of the excesses of German propaganda, currently claiming that the British Government has abandoned London and 'the whole of Southern England is a scene of desolation.' He also states that fewer casualties have been caused by flying bombs that in the Little Blitz earlier in the year.[49]

But this hardly mollifies the general frustration. Sir Percy Harris, Liberal MP for Bethnal Green South West, where the first flying-bomb fatalities occurred, asks him whether the government will arrange evacuation from London for the elderly and young children. Morrison bats that one over to the Minister of Health, adding that 'the people of Southern England have taken this magnificently.'

By now, approximately 50 flying bombs are reaching the London area every day, and although each one may not kill, many of them cause serious injuries and damage to buildings. Croydon has been hit by more flying bombs (29) than any other borough and around 50 of its residents have been killed.[50] The *Croydon Times* is disgusted by crowds that gather at bombsites:

'What kind of natures have such people, who swarm round a scene of disaster like wasps around a honey pot? And is their morbid curiosity really satisfied? Do they enjoy the spectacle of badly injured persons being taken from the wreckage, or... don't they care? [51]

Thursday June 22nd, the day after her previous letter, Yvonne writes again to Clem.

Dear darling,

Just a few things I hadn't time for last night.

Last night noisier than the two preceding ones. I think the wind slowed things up for a day or two.

Awfully nice, darling, to propose our removing ourselves regardless of the cost. It all depends on how young Oliver gets along, of course. So far he is quite impervious (correct word?). Getting fixed up anywhere else must be a superhuman task now I imagine. Don't worry. We'll get through all right. The rest of the news all points to an early finish, they haven't time to knock us to bits that way. But isn't it maddening!

Had a day in town with Oliver at Mother's recently. D-Day, in fact. Went up originally to hunt for clothes but hadn't the heart to buy anything when I got to the West End. Everything seemed perfectly normal, except for enormous queues for newspapers. Charles has been made a Deacon (Masonic variety) and came back early in the afternoon to dress up for the party. He afforded Mother and me a great deal of secret amusement by displaying himself in full regalia, gold embroidered cache-sexe, enormous dog chain and vast purple ribbons worth, we were informed, about £100 in all.

Mother is leading quite a gay life again: Savoy, Claridges, theatres, dinner parties and what have you. Old Charles seems to want to show her off to all his old boyfriends, and he has hundreds of 'em. It's the sort of life she really likes but I know that Oliver has made the biggest hole in her daily life.

Oliver (in the garden today, surveying large upturned stone): 'Look, Mummie, at all the ants running into their air raid shelter.'

More anon. Write and tell me you haven't any news next week.

Love, Y

The offer of moving away 'regardless of the cost' is thoughtful, but Yvonne doesn't follow it up, possibly because she is concerned about money or because the effort of planning and making such a move is too complicated to consider. Additionally, of course we don't know to what extent she is making light of the situation in her letter: writing brave words may be one way of coping with it.

In the early hours of Saturday June 24th, Mr Spurling is fire-watching on the roof of the Astoria cinema in Purley, where he is the projectionist. He witnesses a doodlebug at the end of its glide, hanging in the air above him and realises that if it tips in one direction he will have 'had it'. Fortunately for him, it falls the other way and lands on a house behind Woolworth's store. The sound of the explosion and the blast followed seconds later.[52]. C. Stuart Bailey is in his back garden nearby when he hears the same bomb approach and watches it roar in a shallow dive to detonate in a huge eruption of flames. Fiery sparks fill the air, then there is an explosion and a blast wave lasting several seconds. Realising it has landed in Monahan Avenue where his relatives live, he rushes to the site. It's too dark to see the extent of the devastation, but he is relieved to find they are safe, having been asleep indoors in a Morrison shelter[53]. Luckily, there are no fatalities, but three houses have been badly damaged and others in the roads around lose glass and plaster. Stuart Bailey later remembers a sweet, sickly smell that hung around Monahan Avenue for some time after, either from the high explosive or mangled vegetation, or both.[54]

What was it like to be under a doodlebug as it fell? A Croydon victim described the experience like this.

'The doodlebug's engine stopped overhead and all was still, except for the sudden sound of rushing wind and then the feeling of being lifted into the air and plunged down into complete darkness... There was an eerie silence and the choking smell of brick dust... there was only the feel of rubble everywhere. None of us could move much as the top of the shelter had caved in and was now resting on mum's shoulder. There was the strong smell of gas and just the sound of water dripping somewhere. We were in our tomb for over an hour as rescuers dug away overhead.'[55]

The British strategy for coping is, as usual, humour. A cartoon appears showing a parrot in a cage and a cat asleep on the floor below, with the parrot saying, 'Purr if you must, but don't cut out in the middle!'

Another shows people with enormous 'buzzbomb ears' listening out for the by now all-too-familiar drone.[56]

Thursday June 29th: The Cabinet meets again, aware of mounting public pressure for more information. The view of the military is that the V1 campaign is far less important than Allied progress in northern France, currently fighting it out at Caen. Churchill agrees to make a statement in the House of Commons soon, saying he is sure British civilians will be relieved to know they are distracting the enemy's attention from Allied armed forces. As for the popular demand for retaliation, he notes that German civilians are already suffering far heavier bombing than the British.[57]

The Cabinet then considers lifting part of the travel ban so that Londoners can escape from the doodlebugs, but is told that General Eisenhower wants it retained. A fudge is quietly agreed. The ban will be kept but some 'administrative relaxation' allowed.

Back in the House of Commons, MPs ask for residents of those boroughs where the majority of the flying bombs are falling to be congratulated for coping so well. The answer, of course, is no. Sir Herbert Williams isn't putting up with that. 'What is the point of prohibiting the publication of localities,' he asks, 'when every local newspaper in Southern England at the weekend will have photographs of "accidents" which everyone knows are local? Isn't the whole thing a complete farce?' Back comes the reply. 'No, Sir... there is at present good reason on security grounds for maintaining the existing rule.'[58] Information about the fall of bombs will remain secret.

In a curious aside in this debate, Captain Plugge suggests that after the war the British might use pilotless planes for long-distance mail deliveries. What a ridiculous idea, scoff his fellow MPs, after all, these doodlebugs are built to make only one journey![59]Thus, drone deliveries remain something for the future.

Friday 30th June: Areas of Kent, Sussex and Surrey beneath the V1s' flight paths are now referred to as 'Doodlebug Alley,' and plenty of them are falling well short of the capital. This morning, gunfire at the North Downs hits one and damages it but, instead of falling onto open ground, it hits a tree and is deflected onto a house in Crockham Hill, Kent. It is occupied by children who have been evacuated there for safety. Some 22 babies and toddlers and eight female staff are killed. Only one child survives the blast, but his mother, a helper at the home, does not.

At midday in central London, just a stone's throw from Piccadilly Circus, diners arrive at the Regent Palace Hotel, passing through its luxurious Art Deco-style reception area into the Rotunda Court. Here, beneath a huge stained-glass dome they gather, waiting for the doors of the restaurant to open. They have arrived in good time for lunch because, due to food shortages, latecomers will find some items on the menu are no longer available.

At 12.40 pm, a doodlebug crashes through an annexe to the building. Bridget Darcey, a 45-year-old chambermaid resting in her room, is hurled through a top-floor window and lands on the pavement below. Despite the efforts of bystanders, she does not survive. There are two more civilian fatalities; 168 people are injured.

Close to the hotel is the Windmill Theatre where, notoriously, glamorous young women are displayed naked for the appreciation of a male audience. The Lord Chamberlain's rules do not permit onstage nudity, so these women are obliged to shape and hold a series of static poses, 'tasteful tableaux vivants' deemed so similar to classical statuary that they can't possibly be considered objectionable. Today, however, the No Moving rule is broken when one woman screams and runs from the stage. The bomb has shaken the building, dislodging a rat from the rafters which falls at her feet. Tasteful indeed.

Then, just after 2 pm on this warm summer's day, crowds on the north side of the Thames watch anxiously as a flying bomb heads towards them. It stops, hanging for a moment in the sky like a dark shadow, almost as if it is choosing its spot. At the Air Ministry building in the Aldwych, a young woman is chatting with a colleague in their boss's office. She sees the flash of an explosion reflected in her friend's eyes a split-second before a deafening blast hits them.

The bomb detonates in the road outside. Because of its 18-inch thick walls and steel-framed construction, the Air Ministry escapes significant damage, but a huge shockwave, amplified by the tall buildings on either side of the road, powers through the crescent. Women who had been looking out of windows are sucked out by the vacuum and thrown onto the pavement below. A double-decker bus bucks and wobbles from side to side, its roof torn open. Everywhere glass shatters and pedestrians are speared by razor-sharp splinters.

The grey, gritty fog settles, revealing a scene of slaughter. Dead and dying, some naked, lie scattered among the broken glass and rubble, while above them the leaves have been ripped from branches and replaced by bits of human flesh. Outside the Aldwych Theatre lie the remains of an airman who had just bought a ticket for the play, 'There Shall Be No Night'.

Buildings are peppered with shrapnel, cars twisted out of shape. Ten-bob notes flutter across the road to the shallow pit excavated by the bomb and where it lies, smouldering with a menacing gleam.

Staff and guests from the Waldorf Hotel rush out to help. A man steps from a doorway where he has been sheltering and is immediately sliced in two by a sheet of falling glass. Ambulances, fire engines, police and heavy-rescue teams appear and work all afternoon with the injured and dying. A first-aid post is set up in the basement of Bush House, the building from which the BBC broadcasts radio programmes to the world. The Women's Voluntary Service deals with hundreds of anxious enquiries. Eventually, the road and pavements are hosed down. Forty-six people are dead and 600 are wounded[60].

After the Guards' Chapel bomb, it is the worst loss of life to a V1. But that's not all. Today, June 30th 1944, at least 225 people are killed by flying bombs, with multiple fatalities in Walthamstow and Ilford, to the north-east and the east of London respectively.

Unaware, of course, of these tragic events, Yvonne writes this evening to Clem.

Friday, June 30th 1944

My dear darling,

I'm afraid this letter will be solely about the flying bombs because that is all there is to write about; we eat, breathe and sleep with them. Only two weeks since they began, it seems more like two years. And what a happy, peaceful life by comparison it was before! Except for Saturday night and Sunday morning, when there was a curious lull, we have had them at intervals all the time.

The sirens are fairly reliable. We generally have an alert which lasts all night and between seven and ten pairs in the daytime. Quite often the All Clear sounds and the Alert five minutes later again. We are all right so far, but if it goes on at this pace there won't be a pane of glass left in Purley, at any rate in a couple of months. The devastation from blast is enormous, although the fatal casualties surprisingly light. The Royal Oak one, for example, brought down every window and most of the tiles from every house from the Windsor Castle to almost Purley Hospital. I have purposely kept away from the other local scenes, but even the one in Woodcote Valley Road on Monday shattered shop fronts in the High Street and Brighton Road.

Purley looks like a depressed area again. The shops which have escaped so far keep their shutters up and hardly anyone is seen in the town. All the wealthier ones have fled again. Oliver and I braved the alert on Tuesday and lunched at Wilson's. Except for two firemen we had the front room to ourselves. You can't get a seat there after twelve as a rule.

Monday night was our worst night. Six fell just over the Brighton Road in Pampisford Road, Bridle Road, Plough Lane, Woodcote Valley Road again (St. David's School). I was sleeping as usual in the shelter with Oliver and only woke subconsciously when the windows and doors rattled. And yet, last night which was comparatively quiet, I hardly slept at all. Queer. Oliver thinks it a great treat and fun to sleep there with me. I have given my bedroom over to Suzanne and the babe.

Since I began this we have had two more streaking over. I find myself praying, "Go on, for God's sake, don't stop here!" Doreen actually saw one shot down by a Spitfire yesterday afternoon. I thought it didn't sound like the usual crump. Oliver knows the sound at once and runs in from the garden if he is out. He isn't frightened but he got such garbled versions from Jennie that I thought it better to tell him a bit about them so he knows that if he comes indoors he will be quite safe. I hardly let him out of my sight, of course. I take him out shopping (never go on the bike) and never leave him even outside the shops. Apart from him playing with Robin next door we don't see anyone except Mother on flying visits and don't go anywhere. Nor does anyone, of course.

Thank God there is plenty to do in the garden always and we've had some lovely hot days. Just begun to pick the raspberries, we had the first for breakfast yesterday. I shall keep the little sugar I have stored for the blackcurrants which will be ripe next week.

Your parcel arrived just after lunch and then your letter an hour later. Thanks awfully for the sweets. Oliver got very excited over them. Your stock incidentally has risen considerably since he got your postcard. The idea of your working in a castle on a hill he found most impressive, and he has made several models of it in the sandpit, even with his tin sheep lying at the bottom!

So you are continuing your tour of the Highlands. Seen anything of the fair maid yet? I will get cracking with your socks tomorrow. How about the new coupons for some wool?

The housing problem will be more of a headache than ever now. It is said (rumour probably) that over 7,000 are homeless in Croydon now, with absolutely nowhere to go. And Brixton, Streatham and Mitcham have had it far worse.

I'm not trying to depress you, but it sort of helps getting it off my chest and the newspaper and wireless reports tell you nothing. The news on the other fronts I know is good, but I can't see us getting any respite until we overrun the French coastline, can you? In fact, I wonder if that is what the Jerries are trying to make us do—force the army to invade at Calais to capture the launching sites.

Time for bed. 11 pm. It's not really getting me down, darling, but it may do eventually. Leningrad had two years of shelling, didn't it? Anyway, if we do get pushed out I shall take the first train to Scotland, as near to you as I can get.

Wish you were here.

Love, Y.

This letter is addressed to the HQ of the Angus and Fife sub-district at Craigie near Perth, hence the reference to the 'Fair Maid.' Clem has been promoted to the rank of Acting Major and it seems that Yvonne hopes the new posting may be an opportunity for her and Oliver to join him. At least, she drops a hint.

The previous weekend's lull in bombing may have been partially caused by a change in wind direction, but is more likely to have been due to heavy Allied bombing raids on June 23rd and 24th on supply routes to the launch sites. If so, it is only a short-lived setback because the Germans quickly make the necessary repairs.

Yvonne mentions six doodlebugs as having fallen on the night of Monday June 25th, but this doesn't match official records. The Monahan Avenue bomb, the one witnessed by the projectionist and C. Stuart Bailey and which Yvonne describes as hitting Woodcote Valley

Road, struck in the early morning of Sunday June 24th. None is reported as arriving on Monday 25th. However, the evening before Yvonne wrote her letter, one doodlebug directly hit a house in Plough Lane, just beyond Monahan Avenue while another flattened trees in an avenue called the Promenade de Verdun. Ironically, this had been planted a few years before in tribute to French soldiers who fought in the First World War. The same bomb also caused damage to the roof of a school backing on to the 'Prom' which was still visible 20 years later.

Thankfully, there were no casualties from these strikes, but about an hour later yet another flying bomb scored a direct hit on an air-raid shelter at Bower Mount, Pampisford Road, killing George Norris, a Lieutenant in the Home Guard, his wife Irene and their 14-year-old daughter, Monica. Having four land in the same area within a few hours wasn't unusual because the Wehrmacht firing teams often set up their ramps and fired several missiles in succession in the same direction.

Saturday July 1st: two and a half weeks after the first doodlebugs arrived. The weather, with cloud, rain and occasional sunshine, is as unsettled as the inhabitants of 'Southern England'. Today's edition of *Picture Post* publishes photos of Dover Command Post watching 'for the P-Planes' (pilotless planes) with the text:

> 'The familiar line, announcing that there has been "some air activity over Southern England," can scarcely be regarded as adequate by the AA gun-crews—including girls—who have done their longest spells of duty since the Battle of Britain, or by the hard-worked and often sleepless members of the Civil Defence forces... Nobody in Southern England wishes to provide the enemy with one grain of comfort.

But something more could and should have been done to make it clear to the rest of the country and to the world that the lives of ordinary people have suffered an unusual disturbance. From a military point of view, the attack has been a complete failure. But that does not lessen the danger to the men, women and children in the area under attack.'[61]

Picture Post was a hugely popular magazine and its call for relaxing press censorship doubtless reflects the public's mood; the phrase, 'unusual disturbance,' being an understatement to treasure. Today, flying bombs that elude the 'girl' gunners bring death and destruction to Addiscombe and Thornton Heath; at The Goat pub in Bermondsey 18 civilians lose their lives, another 12 in Wandsworth, nine at a Peabody Estate in Westminster and 13 in the Light Gun Factory at the Woolwich Arsenal, where the roof of an air-raid shelter collapses, burying those inside. In Cheam, Surrey, Charles Bareham comes home from his shift as an ambulance foreman to find his home demolished and his wife and five children buried in the ruins. He identifies each one as their bodies are removed from the wreckage.[62]

Monday July 3rd:. And still they come. At Sloane Court East in Chelsea, a troop of American soldiers, training to deal with the possible use of chemical weapons in rocket bombs by the Germans, is climbing aboard a truck when a V1 detonates at the north-west end of the street. It kills 66 of the men, the largest American loss of life to a single flying bomb, and nine local residents. Londoner Bill Figg witnesses the aftermath:

'I saw this big army truck with four bodies slumped over the back. In the middle of the road there was a head. All down

Sloane Court East there were more bodies than you could shake a stick at. You just rolled over the bodies and felt the pulse. I must have rolled over 20 or 30 bodies, but they were all glassy-eyed. It was beyond me.'[63]

Tuesday July 4th: in the House of Commons, MPs from London constituencies ask Sir James Grigg if he will consider lifting the travel ban so that at least the elderly and those with young children can leave the capital. Sir James plays a straight bat, saying the matter is under consideration. Sir Herbert Williams immediately responds, 'How long does it take to arrive at a decision... when ordinary people can make up their minds in about five minutes?'[64]

Backroom negotiations ensue and later in the day, Foreign Secretary Anthony Eden tells the House the Prime Minister will make an announcement about the flying bombs on Thursday 6th July. Impatiently, Sir Herbert rises again:

'The profoundest dissatisfaction will be felt by those in the areas affected at this want of disclosure of information, which cannot be on security grounds because if a disclosure is made on Thursday it will be just as dangerous as one made to-day. Is it because it takes such a long time to write it out?'

But Eden is resolute: the statement on Thursday will be better informed than any given today.[65]

So two days later, three long weeks after the first major V1 attacks, Churchill delivers his statement to the House of Commons. He aims to strike a balance between giving MPs, and thus the public, reassurance, without minimising current dangers or future threats, while at the same time denying the enemy information it so desperately seeks. He reminds members to avoid careless talk, before describing how much the government knew in the past about the development of the flying bomb. Now, he says, between 100 and 150 of them are being launched every day towards London and poor weather makes it difficult to prevent them getting through.

Next, Churchill produces a statistic he hopes will calm nerves, boost morale and upset the Germans. The number of flying bombs launched so far, he says, is 2,754, and the number of fatalities 2,752, giving a ratio of one death per bomb. Astute listeners note that by failing to deduct the figure for V1s that have been shot down (a number he claims is significant) from those launched means the ratio appears more favourable than is the case. Had he looked at the figures for Croydon, he would have seen that here is the ratio is, at the very least, two or three deaths per V1. Nor does his calculation take account of the wider impact made by each bomb. As Herbert Morrison later pointed out, it wasn't unusual for several doodlebugs to explode in the same area at roughly the same time, causing multiple casualties and stretching rescue squads, medical and voluntary services to the limit. Bombed-out people needed accommodation, factory production could be adversely affected and the general public made more anxious and fearful, so simply quoting ratios obscures the reality on the ground.[66]

Turning to the public demand for retaliation, Churchill reminds the House that as well as continuing to bomb targets associated with V1s, there is constant 'terrific destruction by fire and high explosives with which we have been assaulting Berlin, Hamburg, Cologne and scores of other German cities and other war manufacturing points in Germany.' Then comes a warning. Referring to rumours that a rocket bomb may soon be unleashed, he says he cannot guarantee it 'will be entirely prevented'. However, he ends with a typical Churchillian flourish.

'The flying bomb, Mr. Speaker, is a weapon literally and essentially indiscriminate in its nature, purpose and effect... This form of attack is, no doubt, of a trying character, a worrisome character, because of its being spread out throughout the whole of the 24 hours, but people have just got to get used to that. [Hon Members: 'Hear, hear'] Everyone must go about his duty and his business, whatever it may be, and then, when the long day is done, they should seek the safest shelter that they can find and forget their cares in well-earned sleep.

'But I am sure of one thing, that London will never be conquered and will never fail and that her renown, triumphing over every ordeal, will long shine among men.'[67]

However rousing the speech, it fails to satisfy MPs' thirst for information. Perhaps a secret debate might reveal more? Sir Herbert Williams is quickly on his feet asking for one, saying that MPs may wish to make useful suggestions that cannot be discussed openly in the House.[68] Churchill declines on the grounds that, if a secret debate were held now, the public would think he had not been frank with them.

More backroom activity. The following day, Eden again comes to Churchill's rescue. He announces a meeting will be held on July 11th between the PM, relevant ministers and MPs whose constituencies are most affected by the flying bombs.[69] But when it takes place, it disappoints Sir Herbert, who later complains to Eden that, 'The meeting held the other day was in an overpoweringly hot room, the time allowed was too restricted and Ministers took up too much of the time.'[70] A discussion about holding a second secret meeting peters out into procedural matters and there the matter ends. There is a limit to the amount of information the government is willing to give MPs.

When the details of Churchill's speech are broadcast in the evening's news, another part attracts particular attention. He says he is not 'discouraging people who have no essential work to do from leaving London at their own expense if they feel inclined to do so.' By slipping in the fudge agreed by Cabinet at the end of June it sounds, as it is intended to do, as a wink to anyone thinking of defying the travel ban. Added to his warning of rocket bombs, it immediately puts pressure on Yvonne and Suzanne to leave Purley.

At Foxley Lodge the telephone rings. A long-distance call from Dorothy's older brother, offering accommodation in his home in Devon, well away from the doodlebugs. The women discuss the move but neither is very keen on the idea. Dorothy then calls, asking if they have decided to go. They aren't sure. She passes the handset to Charles, who speaks with masculine authority.

Late on July 7th she writes to Clem, hastily and in pencil.

> Friday,
>
> No time to wait for your new address, darling. We are all off to Exmouth to stay with Uncle Dudley, mother's eldest brother. God knows for how long. So busy and so much to do.
>
> The world is completely mad.
>
> Love always,
>
> Y

Two days later she writes again.

Dearest darling,

We are shutting up the house and travelling to Exmouth to stay with Mother's elder brother, Uncle Dudley. Our new address will be: c/o Dudley Brown, The Chestnuts, Budleigh Salterton Road, Exmouth. (Tel Ex 2435)

He phoned up five minutes after the resumé of Churchill's Flying Bomb speech and said, You have all got to come here, I insist. Very kind of the old boy. Both Suzanne and I absolutely abhor the idea of leaving the house but we have been subjected to a bombardment from all our relatives, both mothers, Uncle Bernard, Charles, etc. etc. Mother has been phoning me and offering the fare to Scotland for weeks!

In normal times I should hoot at the suggestion of passing one day in the company of Uncle Dudley, but I am trying to look at it in the light of a well-timed summer holiday. It will do Oliver good to get away from this theatrical existence. He is behaving magnificently and I shall give him a medal for bravery under fire but I do think he is getting too much preoccupied with bombs, etc. Every plane that flies over he is sure is German and wants to go into the shelter but he is really not frightened at the prospect, he still thinks it a kind of game. The nearest yet was at 5.30 pm the day before yesterday, even woke up the baby in the garden. All sorts of things fell down indoors and everything vibrated for seconds.

Don't like this balloon barrage at all. The ones that get caught at Warlingham, Godstone, etc just stagger on to Purley before crashing.

Actually the last few days haven't been half so bad, a complete lull yesterday and only two so far come over this evening.

Uncle Bernard biked over to see us for tea. Poor man, he looked awful and is having a hell of a life billeted in a village near Henley with a spinster friend of Aunt's and another refugee family. Aunt has cracked up completely over the flying bombs and fled there after only two nights of it, which means a rotten journey for Uncle every day to town and no home life at all. I take a very poor view of her conduct, especially when she hasn't even kids to worry about.

Think of us tomorrow. It will be sheer purgatory travelling with both prams and other impediments. We can't go direct to Waterloo but have to change at Clapham Junction, and what Waterloo will be like I can't imagine. The ban is apparently relaxed for people in Southern England, so I could come up to you if I wanted to.

I have got a letter from Uncle Dudley just in case the police stop me. I tried to get hold of Joy, but she has gone to Cornwall on a farewell flip to her husband, who is off abroad again soon, and her sister in law is staying there too, having been blasted out of Richmond. Pity it happened altogether as I should be looking forward to a holiday with her.

Purley is quite dead. The shops left with windows keep them shuttered and there doesn't seem a soul about. The result is a positive glut of food: cakes, ham, liver, all the things that vanished at 9 am are still displayed at lunchtime, and fruit galore. We have an orgy of feasting, cherries, strawberries, gooseberries, tomatoes, not to mention bowlfuls daily from the garden of raspberries, blackcurrants and loganberries. Really heartbreaking to leave it all behind for the neighbours. Have made 4 lbs of raspberry jam today.

Write to me soon chez Uncle D. and let me know directly you get moved again, you thought you would be in three weeks so I won't worry you with plans until you are settled, but I don't hold out much hopes of a prolonged stay in Exmouth. I think it might be a good thing to find a good nursery school for Oliver somewhere in Devon and for me to find a job to help with the fees, either down there or in London. I wouldn't mind living here alone if I had something to keep me well occupied in the daytime, but if it gets really worse, and Uncle thought they would soon start on the rocket shells, I might even get a job in Scotland, in a hotel perhaps. Any suggestions?

How this war breaks up homes. It might be even worse this time, I suppose. I have seen some of the recent ruins and wish I hadn't.

Just heard the fall of Caen. I give the war another six months, but what six months! I feel about a hundred, and must look double it in spite of three perfectly good night's sleep. The secret is to be really physically tired, the garden has never looked so tidy!

Love,

Y.

'The nearest yet' is a V1 that exploded two days earlier at 30 Hilltop Road, Kenley, about a mile from Dale Road. Yvonne carefully underplays its impact—'all sorts of things fell down.' In fact, the blast shook the whole house violently. Pictures, ornaments and other bits and pieces hit the floor, and baby Michael, parked in the garden, woke because a window nearby shattered and bits of glass fell into the pram. Fortunately he was well wrapped and escaped injury.

In Hilltop Road itself, a mother and her two-year-old daughter are killed instantly. A few houses away, hearing the bomb cut out, Mrs Denise Tucknott snatches her baby daughter from a high chair and pushes her under the table. There is a huge bang and a crash of breaking glass. As the dust settles, Denise grabs her daughter's potty and a few other essentials, straps the baby in a push chair and, leaving the house wide open, hurries down the road to Whyteleafe railway station for the first train to her sister's house in Hove.[71] It is no time to be worrying about travel bans.

She leaves behind a scene of devastation: a damaged house whose doors and windows are blasted out. A little further away, by the Rose and Crown pub in the Godstone Road, an ARP man struggles to retrieve a kitchen mop from a tree, while next door an elderly woman suffers severe shock, her hair turns grey overnight and she takes to her bed where she remains for the rest of her life. Thus is Hitler's vengeance executed on 'Homecroft', 'Gable Cottage' and 'Brambledown'.

Of Uncle Bernard and Yvonne's friend Joy we will hear more. Meanwhile, Yvonne has worked out that if she can travel to Devon in defiance of the ban, surely she can go to Scotland? Her letter drops several hints, but none is taken.

Police on the south coast have been instructed to turn a blind eye to Londoners arriving in defiance of the ban, but they raise objections to law-breakers being allowed to 'get away with it'. So the government bows to the inevitable and publicly lifts the ban for mothers with children under five travelling to Cornwall, Devon and Dorset. When a question is asked in the House as to whether the ban still applies to East

Scotland, the answer is yes, but it isn't clear whether Yvonne is aware of this.

Now that Churchill has made his statement, reporting restraints are eased. Newspapers are suddenly full of doodlebug stories, albeit expressed in propaganda terms. For example, more than three weeks after the Guards' Chapel bomb, the *Daily Telegraph* publishes a photo of the ruin accompanied by fanciful text claiming that, 'As the engine of the flying bomb "cut out" the King's Guard of 86 men had just been brought to attention. Not a man stirred in the ranks and by strange good fortune no one was injured.' The 'iron discipline' of the Guards is commended. There is even a hint of intervention by the Almighty in that none of the altar furniture is damaged, apart from an alms dish, a gift from Queen Victoria.[72] If this account boosted public morale, it concealed much the horror of what took place in Birdcage Walk that June morning.

Guards' Chapel was rebuilt in the 1950s and dedicated to those who lost their lives in the V1 bomb, but most flying-bomb victims have no such commemoration. Even the plaque on the bridge in east London that marks where one of the first doodlebugs struck doesn't give the names of those killed.

Today, the Aldwych is still a busy thoroughfare with traffic thundering past and pedestrians going about their business, just as they did when the bomb fell. Both 61 Aldwych and Bush House have new owners. Buildings along the crescent reach up to ten storeys high so it is easy to see how they would have constrained the bomb blast and prevented it from spreading outwards. In places, pits and scarring are still visible in the upper storeys. At Bush House, I ask a security guard if he knows of any memorial to those killed by a bomb in 1944, but he stares blankly. I realise too late that mentioning the word 'bomb' has sent him down a worryingly different line of thought. There is nothing here to remind us of Josephine Hart, Edward Bacon, George Pittman and the many others whose lives were lost.

In Whitfield Street, the upper storeys of two Victorian terraced houses are all that remains of what was here the day the doodlebug fell. It's early morning and the air is filled with noise from drilling and lorries backing up. The old police station, outside which Bertha Gleghorn died, has been rebuilt and is now used by British Transport Police. Opposite, part of the bombsite created that day has been converted into Crabtree Fields, a small park where oaks, willows and hazel trees grow, and wisteria clambers along a pergola. But there is no mention of the bomb's victims here either. An abandoned sleeping bag, scrunched paper coffee cups, the acrid smell of urine and cigarette ends on a dusty path form an uncomfortable atmosphere of cold resentment.

It's to the Guards' Chapel that you must go to find quiet contemplation. Leave the jostling crowds pointing their phones at the river, the Houses of Parliament and Big Ben; walk past the imposing buildings backing on to Birdcage Walk and turn left at the giant corgi. From the outside, the rebuilt chapel is angular, boxlike and bigger than expected. Inside, in the dim light, faded flags hang in rows high above the aisle. At the far end is the only part of the building to survive the V1: a glittering, golden apse. It stands between marble pillars streaked crimson as if lacerated and bleeding. Suppose it was the last thing you saw before you died?

This modern architecture isn't soulless. In its simplicity, the chapel is a place where death can be contemplated and accepted without fear. It is a generous and lasting tribute to those who lost their lives by chance one sunny morning in June 1944.

Chapter 3
July 10th to August 18th 1944

'I just feel so awfully alone at times.'

July 10th 1944: Monday, 25 days after the start of the main V1 attacks.

A hundred years earlier, most summer travellers from London to Exmouth would have been happy holidaymakers setting off to a popular seaside resort. Today's passengers are simply relieved to be making their escape.

It's a cool day, cool enough for Yvonne to wear her coat. She has also put on her gloves to protect her hands from the dust and smuts from passing steam engines. The sky is thick with cloud: doodlebug weather. As she and Suzanne queue for tickets, they take meticulous note of the nearest air-raid shelter and listen for sirens, hoping they will be able to hear any warning in good time above the screams and hissing of shunting engines, guards' whistles, station announcements and chattering children.

At Waterloo Station they stow the pram, loaded with linen, clothing and nappies, into the luggage van and eventually find a compartment with a couple of vacant seats. They climb in through the corridor, Yvonne heaving suitcases into the luggage racks while Suzanne carries Michael and holds Oliver's hand. They settle down with the children on their laps. The corridor outside fills with more parents, children and luggage. It will be difficult now to reach the buffet car for a cup of tea or go to the lavatory to 'spend a penny.' A querulous chorus surrounds them. 'Why... where are we going. Mummy?' 'When do we get there?' 'How much longer?' 'I don't like those sandwiches.' 'Sit down! Sit still!' A mother scoops a small boy onto her lap, allowing a pregnant woman to step over outstretched legs and take the seat. The boy is restless. Zatter zatter zatter, boom! he yelps, looping a wooden aircraft above his head. Oliver surveys the compartment and turns away dismissively.

As the train starts to pull away from the station, Yvonne reads out to him a notice on the opposite wall instructing passengers in the event of an air raid to lie down immediately on the floor of the carriage. Oliver finds this very funny and Yvonne agrees it would be difficult to do because they would have to be careful not to squash each other. Suddenly they are both gripped by an image of multiple bottoms in the air and have difficulty stifling their giggles. Pulling a serious face, Yvonne points out that however ridiculous, that would be better than being hurt by bits of glass. Immediately, before she can stop it, another image flashes up in her mind: three stretchers being carried into Purley Hospital, blood-soaked bandages, a woman groaning, clutching at the stretcher-bearer's arm. Catching her breath, she turns towards the window for distraction. Peering through the wire mesh she glimpses bomb-damaged London suburbs, Anderson shelters dug in the back gardens of terraced houses, churches, allotments and shopping parades outside which women queue patiently.

Oliver snuggles into her and hums, his legs sprawling and his head lolling warm and heavy on her shoulder. Yvonne remembers the soldier they noticed at Waterloo Station. He had been standing with his back to them, tall, broad-shouldered and dressed in the uniform of a Scottish regiment. Oliver had asked her, 'Is that Daddy?' and for one glorious moment she actually believed he was Clem, springing a wonderful surprise by arriving at the last minute to whisk them off to Scotland. Until he turned round. Now, with each minute and every mile, the train is taking them further away from her husband. Oh buck up Yvonne, she thinks, don't you know there's a war on?

Her shoulder is going numb. Oliver is dozing. So is baby Michael, and even Suzanne's eyelids are closing, flickering briefly only when the train slows at a station. When a passenger gets out of the compartment, her place is immediately taken by someone from the crowd in the corridor. If it weren't for the V1s, thinks Yvonne, this journey would be quite ridiculous. But then, had her life taken a different path, she might not even have been in England. She might have been living in Germany.

Early in 1936, Yvonne was informed that her secretarial services at the *Daily Herald* newspaper were no longer required, not because of any failings on her part but because the man for whom she worked was cutting back on his staff. She was ready for a change. Dorothy, who loved Germany and Switzerland, suggested she might like to live abroad for a while and brush up her languages, so Yvonne applied for and accepted a post as an au pair to a family in Thuringia in central Germany.

She joined the household of Dr Eduard Bootz in Zella-Mehlis; looking after his children, Helga and Peter and helping the family to practise their spoken and written English while she improved her German. Dr Bootz was a round, jolly man, an enthusiast for both the British way of life and Adolf Hitler, an admiration which presented him with no complications. At weekends, he proudly dressed in his Nazi uniform and took Yvonne with his family to various local rallies and parades so she could 'enjoy' the marching and speeches. Dr Bootz's employment was as manager of the local Mercedes typewriter factory, which benefited from investment by the American typewriter company, Underwoods. It seems likely that at least some of this money was used to fund a secret department at the works where Walther semi-automatic pistols were manufactured for the Gestapo and the military, but Yvonne probably knew nothing about that.

What did Yvonne think of Nazism? At the personal level she got on well with the family and, as with many British people of her class and time, Yvonne saw Germany as a bulwark against Communist Russia and Stalin's expansionism and, having grown up in the aftermath of the First World War, she loathed the idea of another conflict. If Dr Bootz seemed fanatical about the Party, perhaps that was just part of his exuberant nature. So at least to begin with, her position was not too difficult but as time passed, Yvonne became aware of the authoritarian nature of the regime and the likelihood of war between Germany and Britain, writing to a friend that the British policy of appeasement was not going to stop Hitler's demands. Whatever her misgivings though, she had signed a two-year contract and felt obliged to fulfill it, so she concentrated on her duties with the family and carried on.

Besides, there was another reason for her to stay in Germany: Otto Kozusnicek. They caught each other's eye at one of the rallies, Otto introduced himself and they enjoyed a conversation. He was clever, funny and attentive and soon they were hiking in the forests, at first with his friends, later by themselves. They became close. In the summer of 1937 they went together on holiday to Salzburg in Austria, visiting the cathedral, named (no doubt to Yvonne's amusement) after St Rupert; Mozart's house and the wood-panelled Peterskeller, where they ate sweet and tangy Salzburger Nockerln and he told her of his hopes that soon Austria would be united with the Fatherland. As time passed and she watched and listened, it became clear to her that before very long, Germany would threaten Britain and war was inevitable.

She faced a difficult choice but, with extreme reluctance, rejected Otto's proposal of marriage. The political situation was too uncertain. Otto was a Sudeten German, keen for Hitler to annex Czechoslovakia: she feared that if this happened war would break out and she might be stranded abroad, interned or even imprisoned. So in June 1938 when her contract was up, Yvonne left Zella-Mehlis and made her lonely way back to Purley. Otto wrote to her soon after, asking her to send him photos of herself, suggesting she join him for a cultural trip to Rome and Florence or a winter sports holiday in Switzerland. He mentioned too that he was off to see an exhibition called, 'Der ewige Jude' (The Eternal Jew) now notorious as an appalling piece of racist propaganda. He described it merely as being 'anti-Semitic' in a way that suggests it was the crudeness of the display rather than its ideology that he disliked. Whatever her thoughts, Yvonne didn't accept his invitations.

She kept two photos of Otto. The first, which she took in their early hiking days, shows him on a wooden bench, wearing a jacket, shorts and long socks, looking straight at the camera with mild curiosity, perhaps flattered by her attention. The second, which he sent after she had returned to England, shows him in front of a crowd at what he described as 'military manoeuvres' in the Sudetenland, presumably somewhere on the Czech border in August 1938.

Otto (left with head bowed)

The autumn and winter of 1938 were bleak for Yvonne but her attention was diverted elsewhere in early 1939 when her Uncle Bernard invited her to a dinner party. Although she hadn't felt much like going, her mother was suspiciously anxious that she should, so she dressed up and went. Seated at the dinner table she found herself opposite a good-looking man, intelligent and, conveniently, British; a senior journalist at a prestigious public-relations agency. He seemed to like her, and on leaving asked her for her telephone number. They met again shortly afterwards and soon became inseparable. In July, when she went to France with friends on a long-planned holiday, Clem wrote to her: 'Would there be a room free in your hotel from Saturday for a week? Let me know if this is (1) to your liking and (2) feasible.'

It was very much to her liking and entirely feasible. They quickly became engaged and three days after Neville Chamberlain announced that 'this country is at war with Germany', they married at a registry office. Three more days later, Clem was in the army. He left her with a letter written on his office notepaper.

> 'From the moment that I saw you I began to love you and from the first moment that I knew I loved you, I hoped that you might become my wife. No-one ever married with fewer doubts or shed his bachelorhood more freely and more happily than I do.'

Yvonne remembers another train journey. After Clem's hasty escape from France in 1940, he sent a telegram telling her he was safely back in England. She had a quick bath, filled a small suitcase, ran to the railway station and, in ecstatic contravention of railway regulations, leaned out of the window on her way to Bournemouth to dry her hair. After a few days together, Clem was sent to Essex to build pill boxes along the coastline. Nine months later, Oliver was born. And now he is stirring, asking her when they will be in 'Exmutt'.

Eventually they reach Exmouth station. A taxi meets the little group and drives them uphill between parades of shops until they reach a wider road lined with detached houses surrounded by gardens, the better-off part of town. At 'The Chestnuts', Uncle Dudley and Aunt Florrie greet them on the path outside their large 1930s' villa with its terracotta tile and white stucco frontage and green lawn.

Over the next week, Yvonne and Oliver go exploring. Sheltered from the east by hills, Exmouth's mild, warm climate has made it a haven for elderly residents. From The Beacon, where the 19th-century well-to-do had their elegant houses, they admire the wide esplanade with its ornate clock tower and pavilion, the sandy beaches, the estuary of the River Exe and the distant hills of Berry Head, ignoring the less picturesque gas and brick works and railway engine sheds. They would admire any view that was safe from doodlebugs.

Tuesday July 18th. A week after arriving, Yvonne writes to Clem. It's a light, summery evening. Uncle and Aunt are in the lounge listening to 'The Carroll Levis Hour' on the wireless. Canadian-born Levis[73] is famous for his talent shows and this evening's episode offers 'happy-go-lucky carefree entertainment based on suggestions made to Carroll Levis' in which he introduces 'The Radio Deceivers' and exciting new discovery, 'Johnny Pageboy'. Yvonne opts not to find out who the Radio Deceivers are and fails to be excited by Johnny Pageboy. She and Suzanne withdraw to the dining room, taking their writing materials with them.

The Chestnuts, 35 Salterton Road, Exmouth.

Dearest darling,

Only got your letter this morning, which was written last Tuesday so things are a bit out of date.

Well, here we are, after a week of holiday, quite acclimatized to the peaceful life again, going upstairs to sleep between sheets and not lifting an eye or an ear when an occasional plane drones overhead. Amazing how soon one gets back to normal.

This is a lovely part of the world. It is queer to think how the flying bombs have presented us with a buckshee summer holiday. Uncle and Aunt are being extremely kind and accommodating all round. They have let us have their large spare room, and their third sitting room as a play room for Oliver so we don't get on top of them all day. This is a very large house though, with an even larger garden, simply crammed with every conceivable vegetable and fruit, even a vine in the greenhouse bearing over 100 bunches, not to mention figs, peaches, apricots, raspberries, gooseberries, tomatoes, etc., etc. Oliver has a grand time "helping" Uncle in the garden but of course his chief delight is to go down to the beach and paddle.

The sands here are fine, and whenever the weather is warm enough we spend most of our afternoons there and take a picnic tea down. Wish you could see him climbing over the rocks and splashing about. I had always hoped we should be able to introduce him to the seaside together, but that's just another experience he's had to enjoy without you.

The town itself isn't particularly pretty. Mostly red-bricked little shops around a green and a very ugly gas works much in evidence, but there are some enormous mansions with beautiful gardens up this side, and a promenade along the front, of about two miles interspersed with well-kept public gardens, even a band playing the afternoons.

Altogether there is very little to contend with, only the long, dull conversations at mealtimes. I am sorry to say that Uncle and Aunt are both dead from the neck up, but so far we have managed to talk their language, more or less. Their youngest son, Peter, is 17 and goes to Exeter every day as an apprentice to a market gardener. He is mentally backward and talks like a boy of 13 although he is over 6 ft tall. He plays with trains all and every evening but, very sensibly, won't let Oliver see them.

Both Uncle and Aunt are entirely wrapped up in their home and practically never go outside their gate. Luckily for Aunt she never has to visit the shops— just imagine, she has never stood in a single queue as all the shops send for orders and deliver everything! She runs this huge house without a scrap of help but even so won't let Suzanne or me do any of the cooking, so that when we have completed our allotted household tasks we are free to go into the town and drink our morning coffee in Clap's Cafe, where all the old ladies and their colonels congregate. So we are certainly taking it easy. I have even joined Boot's Library[74] here and started another pair of socks for you.

Now comes the BUT. I just mean that we can't stay here indefinitely as Uncle and Aunt are moving in September into a much smaller house with only three instead of six bedrooms. Although there isn't any particular hurry, I shall have to make up my mind soon what is to be done. One thing I feel sure about is that I should not take Oliver back to Purley until the bugs are over. Whether I stay here myself or leave him in a nursery school and go back alone is the problem. I don't see that finances allow us to consider taking part of a house, however small, down here. However, I will go into a huddle with Joy when she comes back next week and see if she can suggest anything. If she hadn't taken in two refugees already I shouldn't have any compunction about asking her to take us as paying guests, but in the circumstances there isn't any room. She might know of someone else though.

I hadn't told you that I am only paying Uncle 30/- a week here for just our food, which is less than I should have to fork out for it in Purley, so there is no need to worry. I have arranged for Mrs Juniper [daily help] to go in to Foxley Lodge as usual on Saturday mornings to keep things dusted and to forward letters. She is also looking after Bertie [cat]. I hadn't the heart to get him destroyed. The baker has said he will cut the grass periodically and I have paid him £1 in advance.

By the way, the contents of the house are insured, aren't they? We left in a terrific rush but remembered most of the essential things, I think. Turned off the water, gas, put up the shutters to protect the furniture from blasted windows and put away any ornaments which might fall down. Mrs Roberts [neighbour] said she would go in now and again (she has the spare key) and the Air Raid Warden opposite has this address. Mother was going down yesterday to pick some fruit. Now we are away, I am worrying about her and wish she and Charles would move out of range. Very nasty mess just around her corner last week when six lorry loads of Yanks were blown to bits just as they were about to move off for the coast [the Sloane East bomb described in the previous chapter]. She keeps sending me macabre cuttings about bodies being dug out, just to put me off coming back prematurely.

We don't seem to be moving very fast in Normandy, do we? At this rate the war will last another five years. Or won't it? Haven't had any of your political and military surveys for some time, so you might fill up the space in your next with some deliberations thereon.

Poor you, back to hut life. Good thing I didn't turn up in Perth determined to share your billet, as I once wildly thought of doing. Or would it have been a good idea? Maybe I could have turfed the gardener out and we could have gone in for a pastoral life.

I feel very far away from you now. It must be the farthest apart ever in five years. What a long time ago your last leave was. There was a tall Scots officer on a Waterloo platform which might have been you. Oliver and I couldn't take our eyes off him. I felt quite lumpy about the throat thinking that I had something like that knocking about somewhere.

Have you bothered to wade through all this so far? Suzanne and I are seated either side of the table scribbling away for dear life. I am awfully glad I persuaded her to come too. At least we manage a laugh in our bedroom at times. We went out for a heavenly walk yesterday evening over the cliffs, but oh, the heavy remarks when we got back about a rendezvous with the handsome, bronzed Marines. This place is lousy with them, so you'd better write soon if you wish me to keep your memory green. Kindly note!!

Well, my darling, I will relieve you of this outsize bulletin and hie me to bed. Oliver sleeps with me in a double one and wakes me each morning by tickling and pulling my nose. If this fails, I get a kick in the stomach, and a "Wake up, you silly old fing". Time you came home and gave him some strict attention. But he's looking so well and full of beans. I will get him photographed on the front for you one day.

My love, darling, and don't forget I live for a letter.

Y.

What happens now? An obvious answer is that Yvonne and Oliver should join Clem in Scotland, since it is a completely safe area. Surely, even if his billet is basic, there is somewhere nearby where they can stay?

However, there were several possible reasons why not. One was that the Army didn't want wives around to distract their husbands from their duty. Clem was 40 years old. He had been married for only five of those years and has spent most of them separated from his wife. He knew that once the war was won they would be reunited but, for the time being, he had to concentrate on doing his bit for victory. Then, of course, the ban on travelling to east Scotland was still in place. Whether wives were still exempt from it was ambiguous, certainly Yvonne doesn't think it applies to her.

There was another reason too; one which explains why the travel ban had been imposed on East Scotland. Another secret-service deception plan was in place, the twin of Fortitude South called, unsurprisingly, Fortitude North. Its purpose was also to fool the Germans about the Normandy invasions, but in a different way. Its origins lay in a report made in the 1930s by a British diplomat who had been in conversation with (or, more likely, had endured listening to) Hitler. He noted that the Führer was concerned the British might one day invade Norway from East Scotland and fight their way down through Denmark to Germany. So, to play on his anxiety, in March 1944 MI5 invented an entirely fake British Fourth Army, supposedly based in Scotland and headquartered at Edinburgh Castle. False military signals were transmitted suggesting preparations were in hand and confirmed by messages from the double agents. The BBC broadcast imaginary notices of wedding announcements and football scores to the waiting 'troops'. Engineers loaded up trucks in Kent and drove them to Scotland, aware that as they travelled they were being photographed from above by German reconnaissance planes. During the night, they returned along back roads unobserved, only to repeat the same journey a few days later for another photo shoot. Finally, an announcement was made that senior Russian officers would soon be arriving in Scotland to help plan the invasion.[75]

Fortitude North worked as well as its southern sibling and during the summer of 1944 approximately 400,000 German troops were retained in Norway in case of an attack which, of course, never came. They were only released when a Swedish spy uncovered and reported the deception to the Germans, at which point it was wound down.[76] How much did Clem know about this deception? Quite probably nothing, as it was run from London, but it may have affected plans or activities in which he was involved.

The story about Russian officers was true though, at least in part. In May 1944, 2,000 Soviet sailors arrived at the Rosyth Dockyard to collect a small fleet of British ships refitted for their navy. They stayed for three months until the end of August, learning to sail the ships in the Firth of Forth and how to make new parts for them. Their visit came at a cost to their Scottish hosts. To their amusement and frustration, the Russian officers wore full naval uniform every day, complete with medals and pistols, while the sailors spent long hours filling the bathrooms with steam, supposedly in an attempt to turn them into saunas.[77] How much Russian sailors enjoyed their visit was not reported, but it certainly gave credence to Fortitude North.

On July 1st, before Yvonne arrived in Exmouth, Clem was sent to a new posting at Craigie House in Perth. Here, he would help plan a major Home Guard exercise scheduled for August. Operation Electric appears to have been similar to Operation Umbrella: a test for the dockyard's defences against enemy attack from parachutists or enemy agents. In mid-July, Clem sent a message to the 1st Stirlingshire Battalion listing the exercise's objectives, such as which telephones should be continuously manned, which areas in and outside the dockyard should be guarded, where rescue workers were to be deployed and planned arrangements for dealing with captured 'prisoners'.[78] At the end of July orders were confirmed and issued:

> 'Operation   Electric: Defence   against   airborne attack—Rosyth
>
> '... It is possible that the enemy may attempt to interrupt communications in this country by means of airborne troops or seaborne raiding parties.
>
> 'You will provide a mobile force to operate either (a) in a counter attack role in the event of the enemy attacking Rosyth dockyard, or (b) as ordered by Scottish command, to be at 2 hours' readiness: 1 infantry company, 1 section carriers, 1 section Atkins guns [M1917 Enfield rifles], 2 detachments, 3 inch mortars. RV on receipt of codeword

'Bugbear'. Mobile force 'R' group will RV at Craigie House.'[79]

Was the threat of an attack on Rosyth genuine? It is possible the Germans might have launched a retaliatory action on the dockyard after the Normandy invasion, but perhaps there were other reasons too. Was Operation Electric designed to enhance the credibility of Fortitude North, or was it useful to have the dockyard bristling with arms during the Russian visit? Files in the National Archives are patchy, so it is difficult to be sure. However, it's clear Clem was closely involved in planning the operation and this probably explains why he didn't want his wife and child turning up when enthusiastic part-time soldiers were participating in live firing exercises.

Ironically, now that Yvonne and Suzanne were safe in Devon, the threat from doodlebugs was diminishing. Allied bombing in northern France was interrupting supply lines, and home defences had been improved. The weekend after the women left Purley, the AA guns and their associated paraphernalia were moved at great speed from the North Downs to the south coast from where, with artillery newly fitted with American proximity fuses codenamed 'Bonzo', they fired with greater accuracy. The flying bombs they hit dropped harmlessly into the sea; those they missed were hunted down by the fighter planes, now free to fly inland. Some pilots developed a technique of flying alongside the missile and using the wings of their planes to tip it over—a dangerous manoeuvre, but effective when carried out over open ground. Nevertheless, V1s continued to be launched towards London right up to the end of the war.

It was around this time that someone connected to MI5 suggested it might be wise if the Jones/Cholmondeley deception plan received official backing. Although Garbo had been withdrawn in September amid fears that he might be exposed, other double agents were now sending misinformation to the Germans about the landing points of V1s. Sir Findlater Stewart, a vastly experienced and well-respected senior civil servant and Chairman of the Home Defence Executive, agreed to write a paper for the Chiefs of Staff seeking authorisation for the plan. Thus began a bureaucratic nightmare.

Findlater Stewart wrote two successive papers for the Chiefs describing the plan without giving too much away, phrased in terms that suggested it would be implemented in the future, rather than being already in place. The Chiefs, appreciating that there were political as well as military aspects to any such authorisation, referred the decision up to the Prime Minister. Churchill held discussions with Herbert Morrison and Minister of Production, Oliver Lyttleton, and the subject was tabled for a War Cabinet meeting on 9th August.

They hesitated. Herbert Morrison in particular had strong objections, saying 'If the gravity of what [is] being done should ever come out, there might be most serious political consequences.'[80] Eventually, no explicit mandate was offered, but Stewart was told the agents should send 'deliberately confusing reports to the enemy'.

But that wasn't any good. Stewart patiently prepared a third paper, this time for a more restricted circulation. He began by explaining why the wording the Cabinet had agreed last time wasn't acceptable. Sending 'haphazard information' to the enemy would generate all sorts of contradictions and quickly reveal that the details were phoney. To spell out more clearly what MI5 wanted to do, he offered some simple facts. First, two maps: one showing where all the flying bombs had landed so far, the other where they could be expected to fall if the deception plan were adopted (this was somewhat misleading because, as we know, the plan was already running). Next, he added statistics showing what the difference would be if the plan were implemented. So, for example, the average number of bombs per square mile falling in Whitehall would decrease from 2.8 to 0.7 and in Lewisham from 3.3 to 2.8, while in south Croydon it would increase from 2.5 to 3.1.[81] However, he stated this increase would be acceptable because the population density in Croydon was much lower than that in boroughs nearer the centre of London. Therefore, persuading the Germans to shift their aim six miles south east of Charing Cross would save lives. Lastly, Stewart suggested the authorisation should be worded so that the Germans should be prevented 'from moving the mean point of impact of his attack, *particularly to the north*' [my italics].[82]

At a meeting on August 15th, the Cabinet, chaired in Churchill's absence by Attlee, considered Stewart's third paper. Morrison again opposed the plan, saying the Cabinet had 'no right to say that one man should die because he lived in the south, while others should survive because they lived in the capital. 'Who are we,' he concluded, 'to act as God?'[83]

The Chiefs were now running out of patience with the politicians and especially with Morrison. R.V. Jones later said he thought Morrison's objection to the deception plan came from his suspicion that the real reason Conservatives in the Cabinet wanted south London to become the target was so that wealthier boroughs like Mayfair and Westminster would be spared.[84] However, it is more likely to have been because these areas were of critical importance as centres for the military and government, as well as national prestige. Eventually, a negatively worded instruction was agreed and Stewart informed MI5 that the double agents should encourage the enemy, 'not to shift the pattern of his bombs towards the north-west... he has no need to lengthen his range.'[85]

Curiously, no formal minute of this discussion was recorded, so the only evidence of the decision comes from a telegram sent to Churchill after the meeting. By now, pretty much everyone involved in the discussions had realised the deception plan had been running for weeks but no one wanted to be held responsible for having agreed to put south London in the firing line. So, officially, the decision was never taken.

Still, it must have been a great relief that this game of bureaucratic pass-the-parcel had ended. The Chiefs and Cabinet had plenty of other matters to focus on, not least of which was the worrying news from various sources that the 'rocket bomb' or V2 had reached its final stages of development. For a year or so they had known it was in preparation and that enough had been manufactured to kill at least 18,000 people. Preparations for Civil Defence were in place, but the impact the V2 might have on civilian morale, already weakened by the V1s, was difficult to anticipate.

By July 20th, 170,000 women and children have been evacuated from London as part of an official government scheme, ostensibly to escape the V1 but in fact to reduce the potential number casualties from the V2. Questions are raised in the House of Commons about the safety of those left behind. It's known that the street corner shelters are death traps if they are hit directly by a doodlebug, as happened at Winchelsey Rise and the Woolwich Arsenal, and that better protection is needed for those who live in properties without enough space for Anderson or Morrison shelters. The government is asked to open the new, communal deep shelters; something that hasn't already been done because the government is afraid people will simply move in and stay there. Replying, Herbert Morrison stalls. 'People in Southern England

and London have an extensive experience of bombing,' he says, 'and my impression is that they are fairly sensible and know how to take care of themselves ...'[86]

Two days later, senior Nazis gather at Hitler's East Prussia HQ. One of them, Claus von Stauffenberg, attempts to assassinate the Führer by placing a bomb in a briefcase beneath the table. When it explodes it kills and injures some members of his staff but Hitler survives with only his trousers singed. The British, for whom trousers are always a great source of amusement, find this hilarious; the Germans give thanks for the Fuhrer's survival. So, incidentally, do the British secret services, who reckon they have a sound grasp of Hitler's mentality and want to be able to continue to manipulate him.

On the morning of Thursday 27th July, Yvonne wrote again to Clem, who was still in Perth. Her emotions have taken another dive.

Exmouth, Thursday 27th July.

My dear darling,

Just a sketchy note while Oliver is absorbed in a jigsaw puzzle. He is in bed with chickenpox and looks an awful mess, poor lamb. All his body and head covered with watery spots. But he has no temperature and is in pretty good spirits today, although he can't lean back as his neck is so tender. The worst part is over anyway, and he will get up tomorrow and be able to go out. I called in a doctor two days ago directly I noticed a rash on his tummy. I suppose he caught it from the swarm travelling down, it takes a fortnight to develop and he will be contagious (not infectious) for another two. We are keeping him isolated of course, and I am praying hard that Michael won't be the next.

As soon as the doctor says we can travel, we are going to stay with Mary Nicholson at Tile Hill Cottage, Brewham, Bruton, Somerset. Better address your next letter there. Mary says she doesn't care a damn about contagion and has begged me to come as soon as possible. You see, Dick has been killed after only two weeks in Normandy, and Mary phoned in great distress last night saying she would rather have me with her than anyone else.[87]

In the circumstances it will be a chance to get away from here easily. Both Uncle and Aunt, having bought their new house, are longing to get rid of us all and start cutting up the curtains, etc. They don't go for another month but they are in a flap already and we are obviously in the way. Both Suzanne and I have tried to find somewhere to live here but there simply isn't a bed to be had, let alone rooms or a furnished house. And Joy has let me down. Not her fault, but the owner of the house has returned and is using her spare room.

Over 1,000 evacuees here, official ones, and hundreds unofficial I should say. We might have got a place if we had started hunting directly we arrived but we didn't anticipate the lifting of the ban and the subsequent hordes which have descended on the town.

Suzanne is going to stay another week and will then probably go back to Purley unless Rupert finds something for her in Manchester.

This holiday hasn't been a success I'm afraid. Uncle and Aunt were too effusive at the start and it soon evaporated. Suzanne and I feel horribly de trop [in the way] now. Uncle isn't so bad but Aunt Florrie needs frightfully careful handling. I mustn't run them down as they were really very kind to ask us down in the first place, but even Oliver feels the atmosphere. "Why do we have to have holidays?" he asked sadly last night. Poor kid, the seaside has been a bit of a flop for him, only two decent days of weather for sitting on the beach and he's been pushed miles round squalid streets looking for lodgings. Of course, we didn't know he was sickening for anything and that explains why he has been whimpering so much this week and hanging round me. I won't trouble you with further doleful observations, at least we haven't had the doodlebugs.

Don't know how long I shall stay with Mary, probably just the length of the school holidays until the two elder children have come back from staying with their grandmother. About a month, i.e. Maybe the end of the war then. I can't think further ahead at the moment anyway.

Sorry this is such a depressing letter but it reflects my mood. A brighter one next time, I promise you. Write soon to Brewham. Here's a kiss from the invalid. X

Love, very much,

Y.

Tonight's radio broadcast might have cheered up Oliver. It's 'Navy Mixture: variety entertainment of all kinds blended to suit the taste of the Royal Navy, introduced by "Hubert"', with 'Archie Takes the Helm', featuring ventriloquist Peter Brough and his doll Archie Andrews, ventriloquism being an obvious act for radio. They are joined by the 'ever-popular' dead-pan comedian Gillie Potter who, in plummy tones, delights the audience with his hilarious catchphrase, 'Good evening, England. This is Gillie Potter speaking to you in English'. (It was funny at the time.)

The following day, Friday July 28th, a V1 appears above the busy market in Lewisham High Street, south London. It smashes into the roof of a street air-raid shelter which, predictably, collapses. Fortunately, as there hasn't been a warning siren there is no-one inside, but about a hundred market stalls and shops, including high-street favourites Marks and Spencer's, Woolworth's and Sainsbury's, take the full force of the blast. Marks goes up in flames. Shops on both sides of the street collapse, trapping screaming customers inside. Pedestrians are burned, thrown into the air, sliced by flying glass.

It is the deadliest V1 attack in south London. There are 59 fatalities, three of whom are never identified. The local hospital, itself hit two nights before by a V1, copes with over 90 wounded casualties, but within 24 hours, 100 patients are on the wards. The Resident Surgical Officer reports 52 eye injuries (from glass and dust); 39 fractures, the most severe being caused by falling masonry; and 23 head injuries; a typical list for a flying bomb.[88] Most of the victims lived within a couple of miles of Lewisham town centre. On the same day, at a Lyons Cafe at the corner of Earl's Court Road and Kensington High Street, another doodlebug kills 40 people, injuring 150. Later, a witness records that the cafe is unrecognisable.[89]

According to their Foreign Ministry, the Germans 'are resolved to continue operations without pause during the coming months and, if must be, years to reduce all southern England to ruins.'[90] But the *Croydon Times* reckons that 'the flying bomb has lost its shock factor', which is hardly surprising since 113 of them have hit Croydon, and 44 Coulsdon and Purley. Rumours have begun to circulate about the likelihood of a new terror weapon,[91] and some note that Churchill is careful not to deny this.

This weekend it's the August Bank Holiday. London railway terminals are besieged by crowds desperate to escape after the Lewisham attack and others, and enjoy a few days away from the capital. Extra trains are laid on at Paddington Station and in the crush 29 people receive first-aid treatment. The station is closed for two hours and marshals placed at the entrances to restrict the flow. A newspaper reporter trying to get in is told he must go to the back of the queue. The following morning, his paper reports a 'three-months' summer holiday rush all in one day'.[92] Still, at least those who opted to stay at home have an ample supply of food in the shops, such as milk, pork and kippers.

Yvonne's next letter, written a fortnight after the previous one, reveals that she and Suzanne are back in Purley. Despite an offer of accommodation in Cornwall from Clem, she is packing for Devon again. There is no mention of Yvonne's bereaved friend, Mary, so it's not clear whether or not Yvonne did stay with her in Somerset.

Foxley Lodge, Saturday 12th August.

My dear darling,

Expect you are wondering what is behind the wire I sent you this morning, so here goes.

You probably know I was rather disappointed that Joy couldn't put me up when I was down at Exmouth. As it happened, when Oliver developed chickenpox I shouldn't have been able to go on there anyway, so I was resigned to write her off as N.B.G. [No Bloody Good].

Well, the divine hand of providence has suddenly directed the Marine officer who shares her furnished house to another spot and he and his family are departing next week. There still remains, besides Joy, the owner of the house and a woman who rushed down from London a month ago and commandeered Joy's (then) only spare bedroom, but as the house consists of six bedrooms, two bathrooms and two reception rooms, there is plenty to spare for Oliver and me, and Joy wasted no time in phoning me and suggesting I came down as soon as her co-tenants left, which I jumped at.

It will be far better there with her and her boys as, apart from Joy, her mother, sister-in-law and cousin, also with three boys, are all living in Budleigh Salterton and so I shall not feel at all lonely and Oliver will have plenty of pals to play with. Also, of course, it will make a difference financially as I don't suppose it will cost anything like six guineas a week. It's very queer how things seem to arrange themselves. I wasn't really at all happy at the prospect of Newquay but didn't like to turn it down after you had been to so much trouble. I wired Eastlake today cancelling the room, I don't suppose they will have any difficulty in filling it.

Joy, by the way, is getting her furniture out of store and moving into her own house in Budleigh in September. She said today that I could either come with her too if I liked, or I could stay on in her present house with someone else. Anyway, we can see how we get along. I shall be able to help her with the moving, and at least will not be without a roof over our heads. Merie, her husband, is now a Squadron Leader and is about to leave for the Bahamas for the next eighteen months, rather hard as he has only just come back after a similar spell in Gibraltar.

Another letter from you this afternoon. For once I must be heavily in your debt for correspondence. Thanks a lot for the travel voucher. My old one herewith. It was a great saving on my recent travels. Did I tell you that we can go down to Cornwall, Budleigh now rather, at the Government's expense and I can officially billet on Joy for the princely sum of 8/- a week? Still, it all helps and I shall certainly do so. Thanks too for asking about money. Of course the rent and rates here will go on so[93] there will be a certain amount of extra expense, but how much I can't say yet. May I let you know later how I am managing? I will get a bit of my balance transferred to Budleigh.

Well, I have written nearly six pages without mentioning bombs! Actually I think we must be mastering them, some people who live near the coast say that we are shooting them into the sea by the hundred. Certainly since we came back it hasn't been anything like as bad as the first three weeks. We have had long lulls most days recently, the rush hour is between 6 am and breakfast, in fact the last two efforts at Kenley caught the poor blighters who had been sheltering all night as they were on their way to work.

Went to Croydon today to see Grandpa and passed the havoc wrought by the one which fell at the Windsor Castle. It has left a colossal mess, but do you know Oliver surveyed it all from the tram without comment. He seems to take all the broken glass and smashed houses quite for granted and doesn't connect it with the "boomphs" at all. Grandpa has had a window broken at Warham Grange and seemed very upset and older than ever. Poor old man, he has lived far too long. I wish I could find a safer spot for him. I am going to write to Uncle Bernard about him tonight to see if he can get him somewhere near him, but it seems a hopeless chance.

Bernard phoned me this morning and said that perhaps they might come down to Devon later for a holiday. Mother also talks of coming to Sidmouth with Charles later in the year, and there is also, I very much hope, the possibility of your getting leave sometime not too far off, but please not in the immediate future.

Such a long time since March [Clem's last leave]. I must admit I am a bit ruffled at the instant and firm manner in which you turned down my suggestion of coming to Scotland. It really seems to me the obvious thing to do, and your excuse of getting moved has lasted so many years. I am all the more piqued as Rupert has found a billet in Manchester for Suzanne and the family and is coming down on Monday to help her pack up. They go Thursday also. Still, I suppose if you were like him you wouldn't be you, and if you weren't you you wouldn't do for me, but darling the years go by and we have had so little time together. Will there always be a reason for my not being with you? Don't bother to answer that. I just feel so awfully alone at times.

Here's Oliver's latest. "Mummy, you haven't got a daddy, have you?" (Pause) "Well, you can use mine if you like".

Don't ever forget his X, he looks for it anxiously every time.

Love, Y.

P.S. Quite forgot to give you the address:

c/o Mrs Richards, Coppledown, Budleigh Salterton, Devon.

Send me your mending there soon as you like. Can't do you any more socks unless you provide the coupons. Got your leather suitcase back today. 5/9d to pay. I make the army's cheque OK.

There are some interesting points to unpack from this letter. The first is Yvonne's claim that 'we must be mastering' the flying bombs, which shows how moving the guns to the coast had made a difference. But some are still getting through, as we know. The reference to Kenley is to a V1 which landed at the Godstone Road near Hillcrest Road again, this time on 3rd August. It killed a 67-year-old Cornishman and the wife and baby son of a corporal in the Royal Army Medical Corps.

Yvonne's description of the bus journey is deliberately cautious. What she would actually have observed was that nearly every house on the Brighton Road between Purley and Croydon was wrecked. The 'havoc' near the Windsor Castle pub was caused by a V1 that fell on Tuesday July 18th, while she and Suzanne were in Exmouth. It struck a corner store just as customers were buying newspapers and cigarettes on their way to work. A dozen houses and flats, a parade of shops and the pub were destroyed or severely damaged. It took several days to identify all the dead because no one knew for sure who had been in or outside the store, but eventually nine fatalities were named; among them the shop owners, a clerk/typist called Mary Blanks and Harold Teverson, a schoolboy who happened to have been cycling past at the time.

Yvonne's 'Grandpa,' her maternal grandfather, George F. Brown, dwells in the upper branches of our family tree, well out of reach of my acquaintance. He was born in 1854 in the City of London and his parents owned a cheesemonger's near Southwark Bridge. He started out as an accountant before rising to the position of company secretary of a firm of railway timber transporters, a career path similar to that followed by his eldest son, Dudley. In 1944, he was a 90-year-old widower, living in a hotel for the elderly in Croydon, close to where he had had his home for many years.

Here is a photograph I have looked at many times but never paid close attention to before. It is dated 1937 and shows four people in the garden at Foxley Lodge. Yvonne isn't in it because she is in Germany with Otto and Dr Bootz. Two men sit in deckchairs. On the left is 'Grandpa,' with his walrus moustache, dark three-piece suit, white shirt and tie. He looks like a typically stern Victorian paterfamilias. On the right sits Yvonne's father, the dentist. He stares intently at the camera with a calculating look, perhaps wondering whether the person behind the lens is about to damage it. Between the two, Rupert crouches down with a very young Jennie perched on his knee. Looking at it now, I realise the person missing from the picture is Dorothy, so she must be the photographer. This is a dynastic image: she is photographing her father, husband, son and first grandchild together for posterity on what was probably her 53rd birthday.

Yvonne's letter probably hides more hurt and disappointment than it reveals. Clem has found her a billet in Cornwall so he is trying to help her, but it falls short of her hoped-for invitation to Scotland. Suzanne, a more direct, no-nonsense woman, has probably pointed out that there is no point in her waiting for him to pick up vague hints, Yvonne must ask him outright. After all, how can he, billeted in a hotel in Stirling and reading the propaganda in the newspapers, appreciate the danger she faces living in Purley?

So that's what she did and she was turned down. Her observation, 'Your excuse of getting moved has lasted so many years,' suggests some despair at his lack of communication, but Clem was of a generation where men were not expected to display what is now called 'emotional intelligence', and years in the army may well have starved his conversational skills.

So once again Yvonne and Oliver climb aboard a crowded train and set off for Devon, leaving behind scenes of destruction that are now so familiar that even a small boy doesn't comment on them.

Some of the passengers are humming that summer's hit song, recorded by a British Jewish performer called Issy Bonn on one of those awkward 78-rpm discs. It is a song of simple longing.

Shine on victory moon

And guide our loved ones home.

Shine on victory moon

Across the silvery foam.

Patiently we're waiting down Rainbow Lane

To greet our dear ones back home again.

Shine on victory moon, shine on

And guide our loved ones home.[94]

The train whistle blows, steam hisses and they are on their way again, this time to Budleigh Salterton. Yvonne hands Oliver his picture book and turns to the crossword in the newspaper. I'll never do that to Oliver, she thinks. I will never abandon him.

Chapter 4
August to December 1944

'If I stay much longer, I shall never come home.

Budleigh Salterton has two claims to fame: first, as the birthplace of Sir Walter Raleigh, who suppressed an Irish rebellion, set up two American colonies (both of which failed), introduced tobacco and lung cancer to Britain and displeased King James the Sixth and First so much that he was beheaded. The second is its 'Budleigh Buns', alas, not something deliciously edible, but the multi-coloured quartzite pebbles that form its beach. These are the remains of ancient mountains, washed away, smashed up and worn smooth by huge rivers until they became embedded in the town's sandstone cliffs.

Like Exmouth, Budleigh's benign climate made it an attractive retreat for 18th-century gentry, but further development was restricted by its lack of a sandy seashore. Lacking appeal to the bucket and spade holidaymaker, by the 1930s around half its population of 4,000 were retired military and professional people. They lived in the large villas on the higher ground. Author R.F. Delderfield mischievously characterised the town by saying it could,

> 'easily be mistaken for a European quarter of a garrison town. [Budleigh]... was administered from the Golf House and each prospective newcomer had to undergo fierce scrutiny before he was encouraged to settle. Its politics were, of course, militantly right-wing... The tradespeople used the back streets and dared not send in their bills until they were demanded. Golf was played all day and bridge every evening...'[95]

In the cottages nearer the seashore lived the artisans, gardeners, farm workers and fishermen; the women of Budleigh worked as waitresses, hairdressers and servants or, if they were better-off, landladies.[96]

In 1939, the government's evacuation scheme brought hundreds of city children to the town. For many it was a revelation: they had never seen the sea before and country life offered them exciting new experiences—clean, smog-free air, open fields, wildflowers, woodland, farms with large, dangerous animals, unfamiliar birds in the marshy estuary of the River Otter and strange new vegetables and dairy products. They discovered acorns, rose hips, wortleberries, hay-ricks and sheep dips. Then, in 1944 American soldiers arrived, so much better-fed and equipped than their British counterparts. They moved into the Marine Camp on Woodberry Down and began preparations for D-Day. They drove jeeps around the local roads and distributed generous supplies of 'candy' and gum to the children. One boy's dismay at being handed a can of what appeared to be turnips and carrots turned into astonishment later at his first taste of tinned fruit salad.[97]

In mid-August 1944, Budleigh's beach was still off-limits, guarded by a pill box, scaffolding poles and barbed wire, albeit punctured in places by official gaps for fishermen and unofficial ones for everyone else. The Home Guard still trained on the Jubilee Field, even though their glory days of playing at being Germans in the D-Day rehearsals were over. On the day of the invasion itself, the ground under their feet vibrated from the artillery bombardment along the French coast and they hoped and prayed 'their' Yanks would survive the assault.

Yvonne and Oliver arrive in Budleigh on a pleasant, warm afternoon and as soon as they disembark they notice how the air is much cleaner than Purley's, free from soot and dust. Joy and her two little boys are waiting for them outside the station, Joy all nose, teeth and lipstick, wears a short-sleeved blouse and slacks, the boys are in shorts and shirts. Yvonne can't thank her friend enough: she has more than repaid her earlier *faux pas* of turning up at Foxley Lodge without rations.

With Yvonne wheeling the pram full of linen, Joy leads them up Bedlands Lane to Coppledown, a large house standing back from the road, which will be Yvonne and Oliver's new lodgings. Over tea and eggless fruit cake the women discuss plans while Oliver and Peter size each other up. Yvonne explains that she hopes to stay in Budleigh until the war is over which, according to the newspapers, the Americans say will happen in a couple of months. Even if this is an ambitious prediction, she reckons she will be home by the end of the year.

The following day, Joy shows them round the town. The single main street is narrower than Purley's, but the style of shops and their merchandise are broadly similar. Here are 'Perriam's Stores, groceries, ales and stouts, agent for Caledonian Insurance'; 'Keslake the Baker, Families waited on daily'; 'Mrs Hutchings, Marcelle permanent waving, water waving, shampoo, massage and manicure by qualified assistants'; and 'Creedy and Son, Ladies and Gentlemen's Tailors, footwear and hosiers'. Feeling very much at home, the women reward the patience of the boys by a trip to the beach.

Which is a huge disappointment for Oliver because, unlike Exmouth, there is no sand. The women attempt to walk across the beach in their heels, which reminds Yvonne of scrunching over bombsite debris. They spread out a rug and settle down. Peter, Oliver and Chris scramble about on the pebbles, sorting and building them up in piles. Yvonne and Joy chat in the sunshine about friends, husbands and the war, keeping an eye on the boys and watching the grey waves break on the shore.

Friday August 25th, a week or so later: the news is good. Paris has been liberated, largely undamaged, but its railways are devastated and food and fuel are in short supply. General Charles de Gaulle, French leader in exile, strolls down the Champs Élysées amid cheering crowds until the celebrations are abruptly halted when snipers fire from upper floors at the Hotel de Ville. Immediately, everyone scatters. Later, after the gunmen have been hauled out and beaten to death in the street, massed ranks of American soldiers march through the city in a show of strength, taking the same route as de Gaulle.

That evening, Yvonne writes to Clem.

Coppledown, Bedlands Lane, Budleigh Salterton.

Dearest darling,

Thanks for the political digest which apparently was written a week ago and now seems a bit out of date so quickly does the news change. Don't you love the tactful way we allowed the Parisians to "liberate" themselves? And now Romania out, it can't last much longer.

Having thus dismissed the affairs of the outside world, listen to my news.

I have fixed with Miss Hogg, the owner of this house, to rent one large bedroom and her lounge (the nicest room in the house) with use of bathroom, kitchen etc., for the sum of 35/- a week. (You can think of it at 27/- a week when you remember the 8/- the Government pays for evacuees [allowance]). I don't think I could do better or cheaper for what I get, in fact I am really rather lucky to be able to find such a well-equipped and easily run house. There are six bedrooms here in a row, all fitted with H & C [hot and cold water], two bathrooms and <u>four</u> lavs. Masses of hot water on tap, large hot airing cupboard and central heating later in the year. Large garden, mostly wild.

Joy [who has been lodging in the same house] is moving on Saturday week into her own cottage just across the way. Her furniture went in today and I have been looking after the house and the three kids, so forgive me if this letter seems a bit wild. It is a minute cottage and there certainly wouldn't be room for us too except in an emergency. In fact we have been over tonight and decided there is far too much furniture, but it is all in pretty good condition after four years' storage.

Joy's cousin, Joan, is coming to live here with her three boys. She arrives the Tuesday after Joy goes. I have met her and think we shall get on all right together. Oliver and Peter are a good pair in height, physique and temperament. There hasn't been a cross word between them so far, and they obviously enjoy each other's company. Chris, the second boy, at 18 months weighs only five pounds less than Peter, he is large, fat, very good tempered and brown as a berry.

We go down to the beach every day, sometimes twice a day. As the only shopping street lies parallel to the sea you can do your shopping and then pop down in half a minute. We take our tea down often too, now that the weather is good again.

Lovely walks around, little streams and bridges abound, have fallen for half a dozen cottages. Heaps of blackberries on the hedges.

The food situation is infinitely better here, and if I can get half of what Joy procures I shall be well off. The only shortage is sweets, not a single one in the village for five days, how we are looking forward to your mending!

Budleigh is stiff with retired service people. The atmosphere is best summed up in a reproduction of a joke in *The Humourist*, which hangs in one of the shops.

Lady in sporting tweeds, accosted by Gent with drooping moustache, bowler hat and boots, "Pardon me, but is this the way to Budleigh Salterton?"

Answer, "It may be, but please don't press me for an answer as we like to keep the place exclusive".

Yes please, I could do with some extra cash. Could you manage another £4 a month again? I shall have some big bills to pay in Purley next month. I have opened an [bank] account here[98] I forgot to mention that I have to give a fortnight's notice to leave, also that I cannot stay over the Christmas holidays but anything may have happened by then.

You must feel pretty jaded having worked solidly for six months without a break. I almost feel like suggesting you take a 72-hour when you can and get away somewhere on your own. But maybe you will be able to manage a week down here sometime, in which case we should have to go to a hotel as there isn't a spare bed in the place, but I am hoping that Miss Hogg will go away herself soon, in which case something might be arranged. Just been asked by Uncle

Bernard to try to find them somewhere for a week in September, rather an impossibility I imagine, but I shall try.

Awfully glad you didn't ask me to bring some of your suits down. They are being impregnated with pounds of camphor and nothing but a doodlebug will spoil them. I had the pram crammed with sheets, towels, pillowcases and other linen and simply shouldn't have had an inch to spare.

Did you see today that the Jerries sent over an average of 92 [V1s] a day for the first three weeks? No wonder we quite leapt at Uncle Dudley's invitation. Amazing how quickly one forgets about them down here, and the only shelters we see are on the front. Oliver asked today why they were a different shape.

One snag about this place, no sands. I can't walk barefoot on the stones and to see Peter running along with no shoes positively hurts. Oliver hasn't been up to his neck in it [the sea] yet, but he got a mouthful of salt water yesterday which gave him something to talk about.

No library or wireless in the house, but I pinch Miss H's *Times* and she has quite a few promising books lying around, and the country compensates.

Glad to hear you've been rubber-necking around the castle. Did you find the room where Mary married Darnley [Queen of Scots and Henry Stuart]?

It's now Saturday morning 7 am, and I'm finishing this before I get up. Oliver has just hopped into bed beside me and is absorbed in his railway ABC. I am sleeping pro tem on a divan in the lounge and he is (should be) upstairs next to Joy's boys.

Time to arise. Another hot day in view. Next year we'll all be able to have a proper holiday together.

Love, darling,

Y.

Although we can assume he would not have been able to give much detail, it seems Clem has explained to Yvonne how very busy he has been and, perhaps, offered an apology for having been so curt with her before. With that issue settled and life in Budleigh well away from the doodlebugs proving comfortable, she seems happier and more contented. This may also reflect the optimistic tone of the newspapers: 'Retreat of Germans becomes a Rout', 'German Army in West now a Shattered Rabble' and 'Our little ships bite hard on the enemy's flank.' And, despite a V1 landing in the grounds of Buckingham Palace and rattling their majesties' bedroom windows, fighter patrols and Home Guard battalions are being stood down. Allied troops are now pouring into the Pas de Calais, forcing the V1 launch teams to retreat. Even if the war isn't over by October, the Allies could be in Berlin for Christmas.

There is a particularly curious point in this letter. Women of Yvonne's class and upbringing would consider it their duty to ensure their children mixed with the 'right sort' of families. It appears from her description that Joy's boys have passed inspection—it would have been awkward if they hadn't. But is something else being hinted at here? It turns out that Joy has what might be called an 'interesting' family history and it's possible that Yvonne is offering Clem some reassurance in this letter. Let's find out why.

We'll begin with Joy's parents. In the last decade of the 19th century, her father, John Bevan, was the successful manager of a furniture store in Monmouthshire and by 1911, when he was 63 years old, he had made enough money to live in a house near Regent's Park in London with his wife, Rhoda, and five servants, their children having grown up and left home.

In the same year, a woman called Violet Wallis was living in Drury Lane with her actress sister and a male lodger who was an artist. In the census, Violet described herself as being a 'fiction writer', writing under the name Vivien Wade. At least one of her stories, published in *The Sporting Times* on New Year's Eve 1910, survives. It tells of a woman 'of easy virtue' who blackmails a wealthy patron into paying her a large sum of money by pretending that she has given birth to his baby, whereas in fact, the child was fathered by her deceased partner. Her daring scheme involves her seducing her patron in a railway carriage while recording their conversation, and presumably other incriminating noises, on three gramophone records hidden in the compartment. Violet Wallis appears to have a vivid imagination, a passing interest in contemporary technology and knowledge of the ways of the world. One wonders what methods she used to ensnare John Bevan because, early in 1914 and presumably having been divorced by Rhoda[99], he married Violet. She was less than half his age. Joy, their delightfully named only child, was born in September 1914, so either she was a honeymoon baby or the wedding was arranged in haste.

John Bevan died in 1926 when Joy was 12. Three years later Violet married again, this time to a retired Indian Army colonel, John Palfrey. He lived for only another two years and on his death, twice-widowed Violet became a wealthy woman, owning at least one property in Mayfair and an hotel in Sussex.

The earliest record I can find of Yvonne and Joy together is a few photos from 1937 when they were on holiday in Paris, but I don't know how or when they first met. The following year, Joy married Arthur Chope, the son of a teacher. At the outbreak of war the couple joined the armed services, Joy as a WAAF based in Epping, Arthur as an airman with 907 Balloon Squadron, one of a team operating flights of barrage balloons on Highbury Fields.

But tragedy struck. On November 12th 1940, during the Blitz, the Luftwaffe dropped a bomb on the house where Arthur and his team were billeted, killing all 18 of them. He left Joy over £4,000 in his will and, as the balloon squadron had a base at Woodberry Down, it seems probable that the house in Budleigh Salterton had also been his and passed to Joy on his death.

Two months after losing Arthur, Joy remarried. Her second husband was Francis Meredith Richards, an RAF officer ten years her senior. Was this a whirlwind romance in the aftermath of her bereavement? Possibly. But there may have been a more practical reason. In the same month as her second marriage, Joy gave birth to her elder son, Peter Meredith Richards. It is most likely that he was Arthur's son, given his step-father's surname for convenience; but we can't exclude the possibility that he may have been Francis's son from an affair carried on while Arthur was still alive. Whoever Peter's father was, Joy's remarriage rescued her from any of the social and financial difficulties single parenthood would have brought, and her second son, Christopher Richards, was born in 1943.

So this may explain Yvonne's comments in her letter on the disparity in physique between Joy's boys. She may have been hinting to Clem that they have different fathers, thus reassuring him that her friend hadn't been 'carrying on' in the past and therefore the children are suitable companions for Oliver. Joy's background suggests she possessed a strong drive for respectability and had acquired from her mother the confidence and skills to achieve her ends. She was a practical and helpful friend for the less assertive Yvonne.

Joy with Peter, Oliver and Chris at Budleigh Salterton, 1944.

With Yvonne safe in Budleigh we'll take another diversion. As we've seen, by the end of August she was able to go to the beach every day because the defences had been cleared by then. Yvonne was probably unaware that Sir Herbert Williams was instrumental in making this happen. It's quite a story.

Shortly after the First World War, a military airfield in the Sussex coastal town of Rustington on Sea was knocked down and replaced by a private estate of Arts and Crafts houses. In the 1930s, Sir Herbert Williams bought one of them because the sea air suited his daughter, Rosemary, who was, as he described her, a 'delicate' girl. The house was a Stockbroker-Tudor-style home complete with timber framing and herringbone brickwork, and here he retreated with his family at weekends. He became a member of the fashionable Ham Meadow golf club nearby, haunt of celebrity entertainers such as Arthur Askey, 'Crazy Gang' comedians Nervo and Knox and Flanagan and Allen.

In the summer of 1944 Sir Herbert was busy in the House of Commons in his guard-dog role, barking at the authorities on topics as diverse as alarm clocks, jam and marmalade supplies and the shortage of teats for infant feeding bottles. On one occasion, when he was relaxing at the 19th hole at Ham Meadow, a few locals approached him with a complaint. In 1940, at the time of the German invasion scare, the nearby beach had been wired, mined and placed out of bounds. But was this still necessary? Was it likely the Germans would send an invasion force to Rustington-on-Sea? Their sense of injustice was further heightened when military personnel were noticed climbing through gaps in the wire and disporting themselves beside the sea. Why weren't the public allowed to enjoy themselves too?

This was catnip to Sir Herbert's libertarian spirit. The *Daily Mail* was running a campaign to overturn the ban on south-coast beaches in time for the Bank Holiday weekend at the end of August, so Sir Herbert decided he would support the cause. He organised a mass trespass at Rustington on the weekend of 8th/9th August, which was reported in the *Mail* with mock outrage.

'BEACH RAIDERS RISKING LIVES TO REACH THE SEA.

'Gaps Torn in Unsafe Areas.

'Openly and recklessly risking their lives in some areas which are not certified clear of mines, a beach and sea-hungry public tore down barbed wire at points on the South Coast during the week-end... The public, annoyed by 'Beach Closed' notices at points where previously soldiers and civilians had bathed, yesterday tore down barbed wire and used parts of the beach not previously opened. Here they were taking the gravest risks, for there may be mines still unlocated.'[100]

The infuriated public consisted of about 60 people and included Sir Herbert and his wife, comedians Nervo and Knox, Mrs Nervo, a divorce court judge and the Van Damms, owners of the rat-infested Windmill Theatre. Sir Herbert, applauded as the 'champion of would-be bathers', was quoted as saying that military policemen had been playing cricket and bathing on the beach, replacing the 'Beach Closed' notice when they left. 'This is a most serious matter,' he told a *Mail* reporter, trying to keep a straight face. 'If an accident should occur, the police and military will bear a serious responsibility.'

Meanwhile, he was more than happy to be snapped by a photographer on the beach in his snazzy dressing gown. The trespassers were rounded up by the police and, with the exception of Sir Herbert and his wife, summonsed to appear five days later at the Police [Magistrate's] Court in Littlehampton. Sir Herbert protested his innocence and, as an MP and the ringleader, was scheduled to be heard separately.

Five days later, the *Mail* gleefully described the first hearing in terms of theatrical entertainment. It would be:

> 'a sight worth seeing when the Littlehampton Police Court meets at 10.30 am on Monday. Quite a number of the best people of Rustington have already received invitations to attend... Many famous people in the district—this is the home of financiers, stage celebrities, judges and business magnates—intend to crowd into the court to hear the cases.'

At the performance in court, the errant judge, whose defence was that he had gone on to the beach and 'slipped into the water', was fined five shillings with two guineas costs. The rest of the trespassers pleaded guilty and were fined five shillings each.[101]

However, the campaign paid off. Elsewhere in the same edition, the *Mail* carried a notice saying that, 'There will be bathing this weekend from several beaches on the south coast which have been closed to the public for a long time. More than a mile of sands has been cleared at one town and at another a stretch of the beach was being cleared yesterday.' The authorities had taken notice and responded. There would be no more such incidents.

But Sir Herbert was now a marked man. Back in London, after the trespass had taken place but before his hearing, he appeared at Bow Street Magistrates' Court on a charge of dangerous driving. Apparently, while on his way to perform fire-watching duty at the House of Commons, he had accidentally driven on to a pavement and knocked down a street sign. He claimed the road 'narrowed abruptly' and that he hadn't seen the sign, but was convicted, fined £2 with £4 guineas costs, had his licence endorsed and disqualified from driving for 28 days.

This was just the prelude to his astonishing appearance at Arundel Police Court at the end of August. Appearing for the prosecution was Anthony Harmsworth QC, son of the least distinguished of the four Harmsworth brothers and thus related to the owner of the *Daily Mail*. The barrister had strong connections to the legal world of West Sussex. He seemed to be looking forward to his battle with Sir Herbert, who would defend himself.

After some legal knot tying and untying, Harmsworth stated the facts of the case. On August 8th, a Rustington taxi driver had witnessed Sir Herbert and Lady Williams arriving at the beach and joining the group of trespassers. Another local resident remembered having asked Sir Herbert as he came away whether the authorities were going to open up the beach to everyone, to which he replied 'We hope so', adding that if it was safe for soldiers to use, it must be safe for the public. 'In my submission that was a very dangerous statement to make,' intoned Harmsworth, claiming Sir Herbert's challenges to the law were 'intolerable' because, even though soldiers might have been bathing from the beach, the public could not be assured that any part of it was completely safe. 'It seems to me to be a flagrant breach of the regulations by someone who should have known better. Sir Herbert helped to make these regulations and... he has mistaken this beach for the floor of the House of Commons.'

Sir Herbert seemed to have sought advice on conducting his defence from his friends in the Crazy Gang. First, he claimed that as an MP he was entitled to enter any prohibited area. The court asked him for proof that he actually was an MP and he produced his national identity card. Harmsworth objected, saying this wasn't sufficient proof, and demanded Sir Herbert go into the witness box and swear he was a Member of the House of Commons. Sir Herbert spotted the trap. If he did so, he could be asked under oath whether he had trespassed on the beach. So he refused, and instead offered as a witness his schoolboy son. The boy confirmed that he knew his father was an MP because he had seen him sitting in the House of Commons.

Next, Sir Herbert claimed there was no conclusive evidence that he had ever been on what constituted the beach because the definition of 'the beach' was the part of the foreshore between high and low water. When that failed to convince the magistrates, he pointed out that the order to close the beach had been invalid anyway because it hadn't been published in accordance with the Emergency Powers Act. Sir Herbert was confident that this constitutional point would get him off because it would be beyond the competence of any local magistrate. Anyway, he added, there was little danger now of the Germans landing at Rustington-on-Sea so the defences should be removed.

The magistrates were not amused. They pointed out that in view of his position as an MP, this case was a particularly bad one. They found him guilty of trespass and fined him ten guineas, with 15 guineas for Harmsworth's costs.[102] No MP is above the law.

In September, Rustington beach was deemed safe and opened to the public. Fortunately for him, while Williams had been fighting on the beaches fewer flying bombs had struck his south Croydon constituents than in the previous months, but as we will see, his antics were not forgotten.

Monday September 4th: Duncan Sandys, the chair of a War Cabinet Committee for the defence against Germany flying bombs and rockets, holds a press conference. A dynamic but not always tactful man, he has annoyed the Air Ministry by omitting to inform them when of his decision to move the AA guns from the North Downs to the coast. The fact that he is married to one of Churchill's daughters hasn't made him universally popular either. However, today he has good news.

Standing behind a scale model of a flying bomb, he describes the background to its development and how the government had become aware, from resistance groups and other sources, of its potential threat. He goes on to outline the preparations to defend against its attack and how they had been successfully revised (by him). He ends on a note of triumph. 'Except possibly for a few last shots, the Battle of London is over.'[103] He asks the newspapers to give credit to the AA gunners—just under half of whom were women—fighter pilots, balloon crews and 'our American allies' for their huge efforts in shooting down so many doodlebugs. 'The visitation which London has so bravely borne has been painful enough,' he adds, admitting that 92% of those who lost their lives in flying-bomb attacks had lived in the London area.

Sandys takes questions from the newsmen. To one who asks why such a large number of V1s have fallen on south London boroughs, he carefully replies, 'I think there was a tendency to fall short.' On the possibility of the Germans launching rocket bombs, he answers 'I am a little chary of talking about V2. We do know quite a lot about it. In a very few days' time I feel that the Press will be walking all over these places in France and will know a great deal more then than we do now.'

Next day, the newspapers headlines read, 'Victory over the V1s!' with inside pages giving full accounts of the story. Even the *Croydon Times*, writing of the borough where at least 54,000 houses are bomb-damaged, rejoices at the news, acknowledging as fact the suspicion of many local residents that 'Croydon was Britain's most fly-bombed borough.' Sir Herbert Williams added his few words:

'Apparently we are at the end of the flying bomb menace, and we are free to tell the world that Croydon was one of the victims—in fact, so far as I can make out, the worst victim. I have been immensely impressed with the courageous way in which the people of Croydon stood up to this form of attack. The cheerfulness with which people have endured wounds, hardship and inconvenience has been very impressive. I should like also to pay a tribute to the Council staff, Civil Defence services, Police, N.F.S [National Fire Service]. and Home Guard.'[104]

Later, in a Commons' debate about town planning, he shouts out 'Mine is the worst-bombed constituency in Britain, and I will fight for my constituents.'[105] As for the V2, the *Daily Mail* is dismissive. Under the headline 'V2 plan proves a failure: latest fly-bombs are evidence', the paper's air correspondent reports that with Allied troops overrunning France, Belgium and Holland,

'the enemy has lost whatever chance he had of loosing off his much-publicised terror weapon against Britain. There is little likelihood of the enemy being able to use V2 against England from Germany, or he could not have built V2 bases in France.'[106]

This argument originates from Churchill's scientific adviser, Lord Cherwell. He has always been sceptical of rocket bombs because he reckons they are unworkable. The Germans are using the idea to hoax the Allies. So because Churchill trusts his judgement implicitly, the War Cabinet agrees not to augment defences against them[107] but if thousands of evacuees respond to Sandys' statement by coming home and Cherwell has got this wrong, the result could be disastrous.

Hearing the good news, around 200,000 Londoners decide their summer holiday is over and head back, giving Paddington Station another headache.[108] Anxious to stem the flow, the government instructs the press to report that returning evacuees are experiencing huge difficulties finding anywhere to live. So they write that because so many houses are uninhabitable, people are living in garages, Anderson shelters and rest centres,[109] which is, to some extent, true. A few weeks later the *Croydon Times* quotes the local education committee as saying, 'considerable numbers' of mothers and children are returning... because the government had given them the impression that it was safe to do so', adding that 'some had been criticised in refuge areas for 'running away'.[110]

On September 1st, just before Sandys' press conference, Yvonne writes to Clem on a postcard with a picture showing the war memorial at Budleigh Salterton—an odd illustration, but perhaps there was little choice.

> Coppledown, Friday

> No sign of a parcel from you yet. Have you sent it? Am in charge of the house this weekend, Joy moved over the way and her cousin not arrived here yet. Spent today in Sidmouth shopping, just as full as Budleigh. Oliver very pleased with your card. End of September?

> Y.

'End of September?' suggests Clem has been alerted that he will be granted leave soon. Yvonne's card is followed by a letter on September

6th, their fifth wedding anniversary. Hearing that the doodlebugs are finished, Yvonne, like everyone else, wants to go home.

Coppledown, Budleigh Salterton.

Darling,

Great haste but just to say that if you are dithering about where you would like your leave, Joan [Joy's cousin] has today offered to have Oliver sleep next door in her bedroom, which will mean a great difference in comfort to all of us. A bed each.

Anyway, let me know soon what you think. In any case, I shall come home after your leave if not before. The latest Government pronouncement more or less tells us that we can and they would, I imagine, tell us to keep away if the danger of the V2 were real.

Enjoying another fine spell and making the most of our last few days on the beach. Amazing how this place grows on you. If I stay much longer I shall never come home.

Love,

Y.

This is swiftly followed by another letter.

Coppledown, Budleigh Salterton.

Wednesday 10.30 pm.

Darling,

Very abject at the thought that I completely forgot to thank you for the cheque this morning, must be the result of writing in the kitchen with one eye on the lunch. So here we are, still in the kitchen but with the day's work over.

Took our tea on the beach this afternoon, windy but we made ourselves a nest with rugs between two upturned boats and Peter and Oliver climbed all over them and got coated with tar. Very happy time.

What a pity you couldn't get leave at the end of this week. Plenty of room then, as Joan is parking her three boys out in the village and spending her husband's leave in Torquay. Miss Hogg is also going up to Manchester, so we could have had the house to ourselves. Suppose you can't do anything about it? No, of course you can't, I know there isn't time.

Didn't hear the news tonight but saw the *Mail* today which says V2 will be a flop.

Can I come home please?

Love,

Y.

Summer is slipping into autumn. The pebbles on the beach are sharply edged with shadows and even if the sea is still warm enough for bathing it will soon form a stronger swell. Walking home, Yvonne notices a chill in the late afternoon air. She watches as a flock of birds passes high above her and wonders whether they are flying home for the winter.

September 8th: Sandys meets his nemesis. At 7.15pm in Staveley Road, Chiswick, West London, there is a brilliant flash of light followed by a double boom and an explosion loud enough to be heard across London.

A crater 30 feet wide and eight feet deep appears in the road. Glass melts. Black smoke and thick dust climb to a height of several hundred feet before bricks, tiles and other debris hurtle back to the ground. Eleven houses are destroyed and more than five hundred damaged.

Three people have lost their lives: 68-year-old Ada Harrison, who had been sitting with her husband in her living room; three-year-old Rosemary Clarke, suffocated in her cot in the front bedroom next door, and Sapper Bernard Browning, a young Royal Engineer on leave who had been on his way to meet his girlfriend at Chiswick station. Some 22 others are injured.

This can't have been a V1: there was no approaching drone and cut-out and no air-raid siren. What was it? Sandys, Morrison and a group of scientists drive to Staveley Road. Here they learn that another, similar mystery weapon has landed in Epping. Although, thankfully, the only damage has been to trees, Epping is Churchill's parliamentary constituency. The scientists take various samples for analysis from both sites and within a few days confirm that it is indeed the long-feared rocket bomb. Londoners must now brace themselves for attacks from more of these weapons.

The V2 was designed for the Luftwaffe by a team led by Werner von Braun who, ironically, had been an enthusiastic reader of science fiction novels by British author, H.G. Wells.[111] Unlike Lord Cherwell, Wells thought it entirely possibly that rockets might be developed. In his book, *The War in the Air,* first published in 1908, he foresaw them landing on London and, in the preface to the 1941 edition, asked that his epitaph should read 'I told you so. You *damned* fools.' Sadly, he lived long enough to see his prediction fulfilled.

Von Braun's rockets are 46 feet long and carry a one-ton warhead. Propelled by a mixture of alcohol and liquid oxygen, they are fired from woods in the Scheveningen area of occupied Netherlands, just north of the Hague. The now-famous rocket launch countdown of 'Ten, nine, eight... etc' was invented by the V2 teams. Flying at supersonic speed, they take about six minutes to reach London. They leave no radar trace, gunners and fighters have no chance of shooting them down and there is no time for an alert to be sounded. The Allies can't bomb the launch sites because they are fired from mobile platforms which take only a couple of hours to set up and can be moved away immediately afterwards. The factory where the components are manufactured is the same one used to make V1s, hidden inside a mountain with prisoners used as slave labour.

However, the Allies can bomb supply depots and railways while hoping that military advances on the ground will reach the launch sites soon. Field Marshal Montgomery is in the last stages of preparing a plan called Operation Market Garden. It will be a huge air and ground assault to break into Germany through The Netherlands. He is instructed to continue as far as the Hague and stop the V2s altogether, with the significant bonus that their technology will fall into British hands.

There is another consideration too: the potato harvest. Food in Germany is desperately scarce. There is a huge demand for potatoes, not only as food for the population but as pig fodder. But neither man nor pig is as important as the V2s, which take priority because their fuel alcohol is made from distilled potatoes,. [112]

Within a few days of the Chiswick explosion, 15 V2s hit central London and ten the outer boroughs. The government imposes another news blackout to prevent the Germans from discovering where they have landed. The Chiswick explosion is therefore reported to have been caused by a 'faulty gas main', although anyone who sees its aftermath isn't fooled. There are no broken gas pipes in the crater, and anyway, why would the Gas Board bury them 30 feet down? Wry jokes circulate in London about 'dangerous flying gas mains'. The double agents are brought into service again, responding to requests from Germany for information by feeding them with misinformation in the hope they will shift their aim away from central London.[113]

On September 17th, the same day as Monty's Operation Market Garden is launched, the only V2 to land near Purley detonates in nearby Sanderstead. It prompts this secret report to the council:

> 'The missile fell in wooded area south of Purley Oaks Road. The crater is 12 feet across and 4 feet deep in chalk subsoil. Blast caused little damage beyond that to the undergrowth and trees, together with some damage but easily repairable to a three-storey house of substantial construction erected about thirty years ago and to the north west of the crater. Three heavy and one light rescue parties, 20 NFS personnel, a WVS enquiry point and mobile canteen were put in place.
> 1 killed, 1 to hospital (since died).[114]

The fatalities were 55-year-old Alice Chilman and her husband Alfred.

On September 25th comes bad news. Market Garden, the 'Bridge Too Far', has failed and with it any hope of stopping the V2s. The war is not going to be over by Christmas and it will be a long, hard winter.

In Scotland the Home Guard continues to wind down. Before he goes on leave Clem sends out a few final orders, such as one to all brigades discontinuing their duties other than assisting with civil defence. He directs that all ammunition, except that used in rifles, should be withdrawn immediately[115] and that 'all armoured cars and lorries are to be checked as some may be on loan from the RAF or Navy.'[116] Glancing at the *Stirlingshire Gazette,* it seems the Home Guard are going out in style, as the only activities still taking place are whist drives, dances with pipe bands and rifle shooting clubs. Finally, Clem asks that remaining food stocks are donated to overseas aid and British Restaurants; [117] a government scheme to provide basic, cheaper meals off-ration, made feasible by their being staffed by women volunteers.

At some point between the end of September and the middle of October, Clem is at last able to take leave. It is most likely that he joined Yvonne and Oliver in Purley, which they would have thought was quite safe now the V1 threat was over and there was no public acknowledgement of the V2s. After their week together they returned to Scotland and Budleigh respectively. But only briefly, because before long they were summoned back.

Despite the triumphalism of early September, it only takes a few weeks for the V1s to return, fired from specially adapted Heinkel bombers flying above the North Sea. It is a hazardous operation for the German pilots. They must avoid both the AA guns, now ranged in a belt along the east coast and Allied fighter pilots, who can easily spot them when the V1s fiery tails light up on launching. It is also difficult for them to judge the wind speed and direction or to aim accurately as their radio navigation beacons are being jammed. Consequently the bombs land anywhere in an area from 40 miles north and 40 miles south of London.

This helps to explain what happens on Tuesday October 31st, a night of heavy cloud, when seven doodlebugs are fired, two of which are shot down at sea while five make it to the shore.[118]

Early that morning, Barry Densham is dozing in bed at his home in Higher Drive, Purley. He has been invalided out of the RAF after a bout of pneumonia and is glad to have had a quiet night's sleep, Shortly before seven in the morning, he is jolted awake by an enormous explosion. He scrambles out of bed, pulls his uniform trousers over his pyjamas, runs downstairs, unlocks the front door and races down Olden Lane to Dale Road.

When he arrives, he sees the consequences of the first V1 to land in the Croydon area since mid-August. To his horror, the St Marie residential hotel, which had previously stood at the street corner, is a smoking heap of rubble. Torn pieces of cloth, matchstick wood from tables and chairs, smashed suitcases, even parts of a grand piano, lie scattered about. The lock-up garages at the side are destroyed, the cars inside crushed. Houses all around are badly damaged.[119]

Plaster dust swirls in the air. Barry's eyes begin to smart and his weakened lungs quickly fill with grit. But desperate cries can be heard in the smoking debris. As he stands there wondering where to start, a policeman rides up on a bicycle. Together they lift aside some of the smaller chunks of rubble and rescue seven injured people. But many more are trapped below.

An ARP squad arrives. They turn off the water, gas and electricity; shift the debris and shore up unstable structures. They clamber over broken bricks and glass, listening out for sounds below. Someone brings an Alsatian dog which sniffs the wreckage for victims. By midday, when Barry stops to let the experts carry on, 13 dead bodies have been retrieved. The teams work on all day and into the night, using high-powered lamps when darkness falls.

The final death toll, 17, is the highest in the Croydon area from a single bomb. Among them are the hotel's proprietor, Herbert Warner and his wife, Vera; two young Irishwomen, Anne Brazil from County

Clare and Mary Sullivan from County Kerry; Grace Sword (68), a member of The Forum Club in Belgravia, one of the most successful women-only clubs; and Sheila Lang (27), who had left India with her sister and two children when the Japanese threatened to invade. From her family, only her son, Ronnie, survives. Thirty-one people are injured.

The blast was funnelled down a railway cutting at the back of the hotel, disconnecting the signals and damaging part of Purley station. Some 400 houses have been hit, including all those in Dale Road. The bomb has caused more damage to Foxley Lodge, which is about 200 yards from the point of impact, than the one in July that convinced Yvonne and Suzanne to go to Exmouth. Now, all the windows have gone and some ceilings have collapsed. Luckily, Yvonne and Suzanne had packed away anything of value before they left, but the Art Deco clock has stopped at 6.49 am.

An Air Raid Warden telephones Yvonne in Devon to tell her what has happened. It comes as a shock, as she thought the Battle of London was over, but she is very relieved that it didn't happen while they were there on holiday. The warden explains she must come back to assess the damage and put in a request for repairs. Yvonne calls Clem and within a couple of days they are back in Purley again, clearing up, cleaning and writing lists.

Clem suggests they take a walk up the road but Yvonne declines so, while she stays in the house, he stands outside the bombsite and surveys the wreckage. Staring at the rubble, he is mortified by his lack of awareness of what his wife has had to put up with over the past few months. Of course he had heard about the doodlebugs and knew Yvonne had to be moved away from them, but like most of the military, he had dismissed them as nuisances. The heap of dust in front of him could have been Foxley Lodge, and the thought is unbearable. He walks slowly down the road. Once home, he says nothing, but hugs Yvonne very close.

Mrs Roberts, the widowed neighbour who is the keyholder for Yvonne, calls in. Her house is closer to the bombsite and, in some distress, she explains all of the windows and most of the roof of her house has gone. She and her teenage daughter Patricia are going away to Sheffield to lodge with relatives. Given the extent of the damage and the backlog of work, it will be some time before her house is repaired. Over a cup of tea, Yvonne suggests that as soon as the glass is back up in the windows at Foxley Lodge, Mrs Roberts and her daughter should return and take over the ground floor. That way they will be close to their own home and Foxley Lodge will be occupied until the family comes back. Mrs R accepts gratefully and goes to tell her daughter the good news. Clem and Yvonne check the list of repairs to be carried out and he goes to the Town Hall to fill in the necessary forms.

The news of this doodlebug strike spreads as far as Kensington, where diarist Vere Hodgson mentions it a few days later. She writes that, after a night of 'waiting for the next gas main to drop' she has heard a 'Doodle fell on a Residential Hotel in Purley'.[120] However, by now 87 V2s have arrived and the public's attention is very much focussed on them. Although the V1s are still seen as dangerous, they are acquiring an aura of black nostalgia; after all, at least you knew when they were coming. The Bomb Damage Report on Dale Road is somewhat perfunctory, almost as if its author didn't think it was that important. So, despite the significant loss of life at the St Marie Hotel, the tragedy is gradually forgotten.

November opens with mild weather. On the 10th, the German High Command makes a public announcement. The V2s are hitting 'Southern England'. British morale has collapsed and victory is imminent. In Britain, due to the news blackout there hasn't been any public statement about the rocket bombs but, with the German proclamation, Churchill is able to confirm to Parliament that the south east is under attack, thus ending the fiction of exploding gas mains. Regarding their impact, he explains that the rockets carry the same amount of high explosive as flying bombs but cause less blast damage. Instead, they penetrate deeper into the ground, leaving a more substantial crater. Churchill growls, 'The use of this weapon is another attempt by the enemy to attack the morale of our civil population in the vain hope that he [Hitler] may somehow... stave off the defeat which faces him in the field.'[121]

The *Daily Mail* immediately forgets it ever described the V2 as a flop. Under the headline 'V-2, the Full Dramatic Story: Germans planned 500-tons-an-hour Bombardment of London', its report includes a handy pair of diagrams and a 'Spot the Difference' section, comparing the damage caused by both V-weapons. Next day, the paper explains how the government tried to prevent information about the rocket becoming public until scientists were able to understand how it worked, while at the same time the paper dropped hints to deter evacuees from coming home just as the threat increased. Needless to say, 'At conference after conference, Daily Mail executives strained to find new ways of warning the public of their danger without hinting that this was a new danger.'[122]

In The Netherlands, German rocket teams welcome Churchill's speech and toast their success with looted French Champagne; in Britain, apart from the smart set in London who regularly drink fizz for breakfast, the public are offered 'Champagne Charlie', a film in which Tommy Trinder and Stanley Holloway enjoy 'a feast of song and dance'.

Monday, November 13th: Yvonne is back in Devon, but no longer lodging in Coppledown. She has temporarily moved in with Joy.

9 Frewins, Monday

Dearest darling,

Longest letter I've had for ages and three kisses all to myself.
What's come over you? Oh, of course, it's preparing the way
for the cake tin. Well, I shall be in a position to undertake
<u>minor</u> repairs to your wardrobe shortly, and all
communications should be addressed in future to me at Golf
Cottage, Budleigh Salterton (no phone).

Joy has pulled strings once again and it is all fixed that we
move on Thursday to share a furnished cottage with her
sister-in-law. Only a small place, three bedrooms, but it is in
a glorious position, bang on a cliff overlooking the sea, and
the 18th green is almost under the lounge window. I shall
have to train Oliver not to pick up the balls, nor to play on
the fairway. The place belongs to the pro. (golf, not the other
kind) but he has moved into the clubhouse next door.

I think the plan may work quite well, and in any case it
is somewhere to go until something else better turns up. I
haven't really sized up Betty [Joy's sister in law] but I don't
think we have much in common. She is a Roman Catholic
(Joy says keep off religion and politics) and spends most of
her time golfing and bridging. At any rate she was very nice
to me when I went to tea and said she would be pleased not
to have to have the house alone for the winter. Did I tell you
that she is officially a housekeeper to an old boy, once a C
of E parson, now turned Catholic? They were bombed out
of Richmond in June and he has just taken on this place for
another three months until the end of January in case he gets
bombed out again. Meanwhile he is returning to London to

go to work (another housekeeper and secretary up there!) and Betty is remaining here. Joy's stepson, whom she has adopted, is at boarding school in Exmouth. That is the set up and you will hear how it goes later.

Apart from that, I don't know what I should have done. Just as crowded everywhere. I'm going to try to find a billet for Suzanne though. Had a pathetic little note today saying home was almost as bad as Uncle Dudley's and that they'd had more rockets and numerous sirens, the latter just outside the house and waking up Michael every time. Now that the papers have blown the gaff off V2 it sounds much more horrible, especially as I am out of it all.

How glad I am to be away from the atmosphere of Dale Road. Already I have stopped thinking about it, except for odd times in the evening. Oliver has got his colour and sparkle back and he sleeps well once he has gone off, but he is very reluctant to go to bed and makes all sorts of excuses once there to keep me by him. However, I'm sure he will get over it quite soon, and playing with Peter all day is better than any specialists' treatment. It is a terrific crush in the little cottage, but Joy has given up her bedroom to us and we somehow manage to squeeze into the dining room for meals. The spaniel takes up half the floor space and the smell of hot dog pervades all over the house. But then I'm not mad on animals like Joy. She bathed him in the sink today to the kids' delight, and then we went for a long walk to dry him off.

Budleigh, to me, is just as lovely now as in summer. Still large clusters of fuchsias, chrysanthemums in the gardens and even roses next door. So far the weather has been mild but damp. I bet it will be really cold later on in Betty's house in such an exposed spot.

Lucky you, to sleep away the journey in comfort. I had Oliver on my lap all the way, and the train was 1½ hours late. The usual Yanks everywhere. They are stationed in the village now and provide the inhabitants with much amusement. Don't suppose there will be the faintest chance of a house but I will certainly go to the two house agents some time. Joy buttonholed one of 'em in the High Street yesterday and he straight away took us down to see the one empty house in the village—just a hoot, not worth describing.

Damn sorry darling to hear the news about the teeth gnashing. You've said it all for me, and I'd just like to come up and help you kick the pants of the ones in power. But then, don't stay in any longer than you need. You just weren't born to kiss ... bottoms, was it?

Well, my darling, did I tell you how thankful I was to have you home again so soon? Funny, but I enjoyed your second visit much more than the leave proper, in spite of the bomb. I wonder if you did too?

But in the meantime, let me be your pin-up girl until I meet one of the major generals you are so anxious to pass me on to.

Y

P.S. Another letter fairly soon wouldn't come amiss.

Joy's 'little' house is one of a terrace at the end of a cul de sac, part of an Arts and Crafts development built to provide inexpensive housing for local people. Golf Cottage, which is the house she has found for Yvonne, is a larger, detached residence with white stucco and Tudorbethan facings, reminiscent of Purley houses. It overlooks the sea and the golf course, currently reduced to nine holes because the rest have been dug up to cultivate vegetables.

It's little wonder Yvonne feels a long way from the 'atmosphere of Dale Road'. There is something different about Budleigh that suits her well. Although it is only a bus ride from Sidmouth or Exmouth, unlike Purley it doesn't feel like the junior partner of a larger neighbour like Croydon or London. It's self-sufficient, the air is warm and the pace of life slower. Here, amid hills that seem to wrap her in their huge, warm embrace, she feels secure.

And then south London suffers one of its worst V2 strikes.

It begins with a shortage of kitchen utensils. Back in July 1940, Minister of Supply, Lord Beaverbrook, put out a call to housewives asking them to donate unwanted aluminium items like pots and pans to be recycled and made into aircraft parts. 'Saucepans for Spitfires!' cried the slogan. Thousands responded, patriotically emptying their kitchen cupboards. Lady Reading of the Women's Volunteer Service added 'We can all have the tiny thrill of thinking, as we hear the news of an epic battle in the air, perhaps it was my saucepan that made part of that Hurricane!'[123] In Purley, Dorothy complained at a public meeting at a six-week delay in setting up a branch of the fund there.[124] In fact, the campaign was worthless. There was no shortage of aluminium and the amount reclaimed from the saucepan mountain was only enough for a day's supply. The best that could be said for it was that it encouraged the 'People's War', the idea that even the humblest housewife could make her vital contribution; as if she wasn't already doing so every day. The 'Saucepans for Spitfires' scheme may have been good for morale: it certainly boosted the profile of the Beaver.

Few pots and pans have been available in the shops ever since. So when, on the bright morning of November 25th, the New Cross branch of F.W. Woolworth's store announces that it has a gross (144) of saucepans for sale, a queue rapidly forms. Being a Saturday, all Woolies' staff are on duty, including the boys and girls earning a bit of extra pocket money. A little after midday, the first shift goes for a cooked lunch in the staff canteen while the more saucepans change hands.

Suddenly, at 12:26, there is an enormous double explosion as a V2 hits the back of the store. This is followed by a moment of complete silence, then the walls bow and buckle and the whole building collapses. Outside, the blast wave concertinas a passing No. 53 bus, its passengers killed by blast trauma to their internal organs while they are still sitting upright.

It's yet another appalling scene of devastation. It takes three days to clear the debris and recover all the bodies. Rumours circulate about body parts being offered to relatives for identification and a fireman, one of the first rescuers to arrive on the scene, suffers nightmares for years afterwards. Some 168 people are dead; 121 are injured, most of them inside Woolworth's and the Co-Operative store next door. It is the largest loss of life to a single V2.

December. This Christmas is the sixth since the start of hostilities. At Covent Garden, Christmas trees are on sale at a shilling a foot. In the House of Commons, Sir Herbert Williams is on his feet again, asking whether, given the shortage of toilet paper, the government could have the supply increased? Should the scheme for assisted migration, currently being discussed with dominion governments, be referred to in future as 'the flight from Beveridge'? (Sir Herbert objects to the

Beveridge Report, which sets out new arrangements for social services, and votes against it.)[125]

On December 8th, a Ministry of Food cook on 'The Kitchen Front' programme describes how a Christmas pudding can be made from soya flour, suet, breadcrumbs, dried egg, grated carrots and apples, with the additional treat of dates stuffed with margarine and almond essence. Later, Oliver listens to 'Children's Hour: The Magic Bed-Knob, or how to become a witch in three easy lessons, by Mary Norton, with Margaret Rutherford.' It seems the author of *The Borrowers* wrote the first draft of Harry Potter.

That evening Yvonne writes to Clem. Either it is the first letter for a month or an intervening one has been lost.

Golf Cottage, Budleigh Salterton,

8th December 1944.

Darling,

Hope you get the apples this week. They weighed 16 lbs, i.e. 1 lb overweight for the post office so I had to lug them all the way to the railway station. They said they would only take about two days to get there. I put in one or two Coxs from a box Charles sent me, but couldn't get anything like as good for you, but they seemed better than your last lot to me.

Well, we're still here but have got to move on again after Xmas when Betty's old hypochondriac comes down for the last three weeks of his tenancy. He will bring his secretary too, and as Anthony will still be here on holiday there simply won't be room for us.

I am beginning to worry as to what I shall do if no rooms or boarding houses become available. I don't want to have to appeal to Joy again. Living on people's kindness indefinitely is a strain and anyway I hate Joy's horrible mangey spaniel who has given both her children worms and might contaminate Oliver.

Betty and I are getting on quite well, better than I hoped and, I imagine, better than she and Joy do. She is going to marry an old boy of 65 who comes to tea three times a week. He is a solicitor at Exeter and has an office too in Budleigh. I am getting quite a discreet gooseberry and remember to cough loudly before entering the room. They hold hands under the table and eventually disappear into her bedroom with vague excuses. I am all for young love, but this seems a bit queer. However, I think Betty is genuinely fond of him but God knows why she doesn't look for someone nearer her age, thirty-eight. She was married at eighteen to a bank clerk who has been to prison several times for embezzlement, and although she is very fond of talking about life I don't think she knows much about it. All the old men of Budleigh adore her and queue up to stand her coffees and she knows and relates to me all the local scandal. I've no doubt that everyone has heard all about me, what there is!

This little house is the coldest ever. The wind whistles round the walls at night like the noises off in a ghost play, but the views from all sides are magnificent—the golf course, the sea and the open country. I never knew the sea could vary like this, it never looks the same colour from day to day and we get the most heavenly sunsets and early morning skies. The house itself is very poorly furnished and not very comfortable, nothing fits and all the doors and drawers stick, much to Oliver's annoyance. The beds are quite frightful—mine is like a hammock—and the pictures too, we actually have the Stag at Bay in the lounge. Stickley, the golf pro., is dying from cancer in the clubhouse and when he finally does Mrs Stickley wants to come back here and so won't renew the tenancy in January.

Oliver and I generally walk down to the shops along the cliffs and bus back part of the way. Afternoon walks are a real pleasure and we go to tea with Joan and Joy quite a bit, and they come here when Betty is out. Otherwise the only excitement is lunch at Exmouth where I change the library book and hunt desperately for Xmas presents. I started to buy some bits of nonsense for the stocking but Oliver found them in the wardrobe, so now I must start again or destroy his faith in the Santa Claus legend. Xmas will be simply bloody, but at least he hasn't many comparisons to make.

Sorry I haven't written before, but I wasn't very well. Have fixed to swap the whiskey for a bottle of gin when it arrives.

Never been so depressed about the war.

Y.

She's not alone. Disappointment at the lack of an end to the war is harder to bear after the eager optimism of late summer. But even if rations are short and their streets wrecked, the British will keep plodding on because the war is still going their way.

It seems Yvonne knows more about Betty's circumstances than she is prepared to put in writing, as she diplomatically avoids spelling out her co-tenant's relationships. Mary Elizabeth ('Betty') is the younger sister of Joy's husband, Frances Meredith Richards. In 1928, she married

Leonard Hall in Kingston-upon-Thames. How he managed to be employed by various banks after spending time in prison for embezzlement is an interesting question but, by the outbreak of war, Betty is no longer with him. She is registered as being 'housekeeper/chauffeuse' to the Reverend Frederick Chambers in Twickenham, living in his house with her son and his other staff. There is no sign of Leonard but it is possible that he may have left Betty ten years earlier and gone to live in Canada.

Anyone suffering from flu, as Yvonne has, would not have had to look far for remedies. The newspapers are full of advertisements for Aspro, Beecham's Powders and Dr J. Collis Browne's well-known 'Chlorodyne: Unrivalled for Coughs, Colds, Catarrh, Asthma, Bronchitis, Neuralgia, Gout, Rheumatism, Toothache. Acts like a charm in Diarrhoea, Stomach Chills. 1s 5d at all chemists', which is made from peppermint-flavoured morphine. And with wartime meals relying heavily on stodgy food like root vegetables, there is a need for digestive treatments such as 'Nightly Bile Beans' or 'Pinkettes Liver Pills for the sluggish liver, flatulence, a coated tongue and bad breath... Small in size! Effective in action!'

But even these claims are outstripped by those for Kruschen Salts. This was a mixture of salts and citric acid, a testimonial for which appears in the *Devon and Exeter Gazette* under the heading 'Boiled the Kettle with his Crutches':

> 'For five years I was a cripple due to rheumatism and was given up as a hopeless case. I also had a bad stomach and I could never enjoy a meal without my food repeating on me. One day an old friend of mine told me to try Kruschen Salts. So I bought a bottle and gave it a trial. After taking two bottles I was able to sit down and enjoy a good meal. I was also getting about more freely. One morning I got up and lit

the fire. My mother thought I was crazy because I sawed my old crutches up and boiled the kettle with them. That was six years ago and I am now back at my old job as a chef.'[126]

Kruschen Salts have since been replaced by Rennies, whose results are less dramatic,

As Christmas approaches, the last restrictions on travelling to the south coast are lifted and as a result the railways are busier than at a summer Bank Holiday. For instance, the queue at Waterloo Station for trains to Bournemouth and Weymouth stretches out of the station and down the approach road. Troops and Italian prisoners of war are brought in to help shift seasonal freight, which presumably includes the apples Yvonne has sent to Clem.[127]

In Budleigh, the town does its best to celebrate the festive season with shop window displays, dances, whist drives, carol singing and children's parties organised by the churches. The Americans put on a film show for the children at the Public Hall and plenty of the much-desired 'candy' is handed out. Perhaps Oliver and the Richards boys were among the happy recipients.

Yvonne's next letter is more breathlessly cheerful than the last.

Golf Cottage, Budleigh Salterton. 21st December 1944

My darling,

At last, a relatively quiet evening to get my breath back. Everything's been a rush, but I'll explain.

You see, Betty and Dudley suddenly decided to get married at the off licence in Exeter yesterday. His housekeeper had walked out after he gave her a month's notice and as there was nobody to look after him so it seemed the obvious solution! Thank heavens they've done it at last, I was getting rather worn with being drawn into all the developments. I even composed a letter breaking the news to Dudley's step-daughter in India! Ah well, now we can all relax. They are coming back here tomorrow afternoon and will stay over the holidays and then, I suppose, go back to Dudley's house in Exeter. Meantime, I am looking after Antony, Betty's adopted son. He is a tall but babyish seven years old. Oliver thinks he is the cat's pyjamas and copies him in every way, even to calling me "Auntie"!

We went over to Exmouth this afternoon to collect the photos of Oliver. They are really awfully good, I think, and I shall order some more copies. Have only three so far, so if I send one to each of the Grannies we must share one pro tem; that is, when you've had a good look at yours, you can send it back for me to file until we have our own mantelpiece again. I could get you a postcard size if you like, to carry about. Let me know.

Your large parcel for Oliver has arrived and is hidden away
for the day. It looks most exciting. All very well for you
to suggest ignoring Xmas, you could do so if you had only
yourself to think about, but not with children. Oliver can
hardly wait and keeps asking me when it is and will we be
able to wear paper hats. I've got mother to send down the
box of our usual decorations, helped myself to holly from
the golf course and have big ideas for special treats to eat.
Betty has a chicken and Dudley has ordered a goose, so we
shan't starve. But we've no drink, and I'm hoping that your
promised bottle will turn up soon, or have you changed your
mind and drunk it yourself?

Somehow I feel you won't be able to defy the travel ban, but I'm hoping desperately and holding my thumbs. It would be so lovely to have you here for Xmas, the first for four years, and I'm sure you'd like it. We shall have fires going in both rooms so that we wouldn't be de trop. I expect I shall, as usual, do most of the cooking and housework. Betty is kind and has her points but she is damn lazy and untidy. However, she has taken me in and is very sweet with Oliver. So is Dudley too—he is talking of taking us all to the pantomime in Exeter next month.

I haven't written to the addresses you gave me as this marriage alters the situation completely. There is a good chance that Mr Chambers won't come down now that Betty won't be here, in which case I'm hoping he will let me take over the cottage for January. It would be worth paying 3 guineas a week for a month if you are getting ten days' leave, and I might even persuade Mrs Stickley to let me keep it on, or part of it, after January. In any case, I'd rather stay on to the last, and even if we have to go I have found a woman in Victoria Place who thinks she could let me have a couple of rooms after Xmas.

So you see, the situation isn't so frantic as when I last wrote. Thanks awfully for all the help. I'm afraid I got you worried but I was feeling rather down after the bout of flu and felt depressed. Now we are settled in Budleigh with friends for Oliver and me I don't want to have to move elsewhere, even for a few miles, if I can help it. I still search the front page of the Western Morning News every day but don't see how, even if there should be a suitable cottage, I should be able to organise an inspection. These places get snapped up at once and are mostly in remote spots. But I loathe the idea of having to return one day to the shoddy suburbanism of Purley, don't you?

Mother visited Foxley Lodge last week and has managed to arrange for windows to be put back in the dining room this week. Mrs Roberts has returned from Sheffield, which is a good thing in a way as she will see the place is kept clean. The geyser went wrong and has been taken away.

Just seen the death of a youthful admirer in the Times today, killed in Greece. How very unnecessary in a way to have to die. Wish I could acquire your optimism about the war. Thank goodness the wireless has completely conked out and there will be no newspapers for two days. I shall imitate the ostrich.

You asked about rockets and wonder if London still gets them. Don't you ever hear rumours of the horrible things? One fell on a Woolworths in New Cross Gate and killed 100 women and children queuing up for the first ice creams.[128] Another doodlebug came down at the back of Selfridges and a rocket in Battersea across the river by mother. Is Scotland really a country which doesn't know there is a war? I'm always hearing so.

Heard from Uncle Bernard today. They are spending Xmas in the Isle of Wight. He sent Oliver an "insignificant" cheque (two guineas) which I shall bank and not spend on a piece of wood with nails knocked in.

I have at last bought myself a new dress. It is olive green and rather dull, but <u>warm</u>! Was overjoyed to learn that I had yet another six coupons hidden at the back, so you may with luck see me in skirts and not my hideous trousers next time, provided I can find some decent stockings.

Sorry, but Oliver hasn't any idea of counting beyond four. But he knows all his letters which is more than Peter or Nigel do. So, you could read at three, could you? It only shows how these infant prodigies fade out later, doesn't it! In any case, after looking at the photos again, I'm sure he'll have the pick of all the world's heiresses and won't have to work for his living.

What's the story about the pig who wanted to cross the river? He keeps asking me to tell it. And how, please, do you make paper aeroplanes? Just a sheet folded somehow, I think.

Love and lots more,

Y.

Perhaps if the Reverend Chambers was carrying on with his secretary in Richmond-upon-Thames, Betty felt free to do the same with Dudley in Budleigh. Or did Yvonne's presence at Golf Cottage galvanise them into marriage?

There is something odd about the reference to the 'youthful admirer' who has lost his life. He is Lieutenant Rex Willson of the Royal Tank Regiment. The *Times* and the Commonwealth War Graves Commission give his age as 23. If that is so, he was ten years younger than Yvonne and means that at the outbreak of war she was 28 and he was 18, so he would have been a very youthful admirer.

'Back of Selfridges' refers to a V2 strike which took place on 6th December. It hit the Red Lion pub close to the famous department store and blew a Christmas tree across Oxford Street. Eight American servicemen were killed and 32 injured; ten British civilians also died. The Battersea V2 she mentions is one which fell on open ground close to midnight on November 21st causing five fatalities.

Christmas Eve is the coldest night for more than half a century. 'Southern England' enjoys respite from the flying bombs, instead Manchester is the target. From above the Yorkshire coast, 45 doodlebugs are fired at the city, many of which land harmlessly. However, in Oldham 27 people, including several children, are killed.

One curiosity of this attack is yet another attempt by the Germans to pinpoint where the doodlebugs had landed. The Manchester bombs contained leaflets headed 'V1 Post', which purported to be a 'special Christmas' delivery. They included images of letters written by hospitalised British Prisoners of War to their loved ones at home. Whoever picked up a leaflet was encouraged to cut it out or copy the image and send it to the person to whom it had been addressed. If the addressee replied to the prisoner, their letter would be intercepted by German censors who, through a system of code numbers included in the correspondence, would be able to work out where the leaflet had originally been retrieved. The British police collected up most of the leaflets and warned the addressees, thus preventing replies being sent.[129]

Christmas Day is frosty. At Golf Cottage the tree stands in the sitting room, decorated with ornaments sent from Purley and the extra ones Yvonne and Oliver have made together from newspaper, cotton reels and fir cones. Oliver is as excited by the government's extra sweet ration for children as he is by Santa's ability to find him in Devon and leave him a stocking full of goodies. They wrap up in coats, hats, scarves and gloves and go down to the hill to St Peter's Church, a large Victorian building bearing the scars of German bombing before returning for lunch of roast chicken or goose and the special treats Yvonne has prepared. Joy and her boys join them for the afternoon, so it's time to open their presents and listen to King George VI's radio broadcast, one in which he hopes for 'a world of free men, untouched by tyranny.' The speech is a huge achievement for him, being the first he has delivered without the assistance of his speech therapist. This is followed by the National Anthems of all the Allies, which takes a considerable time to play through. That evening, after the guests have left and Oliver is in bed, Yvonne listens to a variety show on the wireless, starring comedians Kenneth Horne, Richard Murdoch, sisters Elsie and Doris Waters and aficionado of the Ham Golf Club Arthur Askey.

In Croydon, Sir Herbert Williams has sent his own Christmas message to his constituents:

> '...Croydon has gone through many difficulties in the last five and a half years and certainly the worst of all of them was the period of the heavy flying bomb raids. The fact that, during that trying time, there was never the faintest sign of a break of morale is the best possible tribute to the stout-heartedness of the citizens of Croydon. I hope that 1945 may be the year of Peace, and that it will be possible rapidly to repair the ravages of war.'[130]

The Germans suspend all V2 firings for Christmas Day, but normal service is resumed on Boxing Day when four are launched. One hits The Prince of Wales pub in Islington, killing 73 people. Three days later, one of the few V2s to land in Croydon explodes above Croham Valley Road, killing Air Raid Warden Gertrude Jackson, her Home Guard officer husband and another resident. It damages 2,000 houses.

Earlier in the year when Dorothy took Yvonne and Oliver to London Zoo, they would have seen one of its main attractions: Ming, the popular panda. Described as '200lbs of lovable mischievousness', she had amused countless visitors, especially children, with her cute antics; so much so that she became a poster girl for the zoo. Her picture appeared in advertisements and on merchandise, beguiling parents into buying brooches, toys and tins of biscuits for their children. Unfortunately, as was the case with zoos in those days, Ming was housed in conditions that were far from ideal and was often made to 'perform' for the public by wearing hats, sitting on chairs and so on.

In 1939 some of the zoo's most precious animals were evacuated to Whipsnade Zoo while the venomous ones were killed in case they escaped during a bombing raid. Ming, a star celebrity, remained in London and during the Blitz her image was reinvented from 'playful cub' to 'resolute heroine' so that children under fire had a comforting role model to look up to. Sadly, by 1944 her health was deteriorating and on Boxing Day she died. Ming was rewarded with an obituary in *The Times* and by being stuffed by a London taxidermist who then made a small fortune touring her remains around the country. [131]

Chapter 5
January to August 1945

'Suddenly it came to me how happy I was, more so than I'd been for years

and perhaps likely to be for years to come.

January 1st 1945: Monday.

The new year brings fresh hope. At least to some. For Churchill, 1945 is 'this new, disgusting year.'[132]Britain is fog-bound, frosty and cold. Households have been instructed to restrict their use of coal, gas and electricity to prevent shortages for the war industries.

Hitler addresses the German nation on the wireless. He hasn't been seen or heard from in public since the attempt on his life last summer, but has decided to appear today because a recent, colossal assault on Allied troops in the Ardennes Forest has convinced him that he can still win the war. In his speech, he promises his people they will never be defeated by 'bourgeois parliamentary-democratic half-measures', threatening that anyone who thinks otherwise will be destroyed. He thanks them for their efforts and gives a nod to the Almighty too for his support.[133] However, once the fog clears and skies in France are open for business, Allied planes can fly again. The threatened attack fails.

Hitler's grip on reality is weak, but no one in his inner circle dare tell him the truth: that he is losing the war. Germany, its industry, infrastructure and cities, is being flattened. Hamburg and Berlin are in flames. Allied planes are bombing German oil refineries; everywhere people are short of food, fuel and water. Nonetheless, V1s and V2s are still being fired from the Netherlands and Hitler still believes they will bring him victory. Little does he know that Wernher von Braun has already decided to surrender himself and his team of 112 scientists to the Americans, along with their rocket plans and equipment.

The *Devon and Exeter Gazette* reports Hitler's speech, describing him as 'sullen but still fanatical in his belief in himself as Europe's man of destiny and in his own twisted version of history.'[134] Yvonne reads this with weary contempt and turns the page in search of something more cheerful. What's on at the cinema? Well, there's a choice between Laurence Olivier's morale-boosting, technicolour Shakespearian epic, *Henry V* and *The Mask of Dimitrios*, a thriller about a mysterious body washed up in Istanbul. It seems the screenwriters lacked the Bard's imagination in naming the characters in this film, because Peter Lorre stars as The Little Man and Sidney Greenstreet as The Fat Man. Still, at least his catchphrase 'There's not enough kindness in the world' rings true.

As New Year's Day closes, Yvonne and Oliver listen to a live broadcast performance of a pantomime, after which Oliver is tucked up in bed and Yvonne settles down to write to Clem. She is on the move again.

Golf Cottage, Budleigh Salterton

Monday 1.1.45.

My darling,

Well, it's fixed that we leave here on Saturday afternoon for 17 Victoria Place. Please note the address, and don't send letters to Prince Albert Terrace. We are only going for three weeks, I hope, and then coming back here, but I still can't get Mrs Stickley to make up her mind about letting. She burst into tears last time I tried to pin her down so we shall just have to go carefully.

We are going to "apartments"—one twin-bedded room, very cold and sparse, and one minute, grim, pokey sitting room about the size of Suzanne's kitchen, for which I shall have to pay 3½ guineas a week and buy my own food. Of course, it would be beyond my means indefinitely, but there is absolutely no other else in Budleigh, either in the way of rooms or at guest houses. If this cottage falls through I shall look for cheaper but, I hope, pleasanter rooms. Leave there would be just possible for you, I think, although a comedown from the Golden Lion[135], but I'm really hoping to be back here for that.

Blast Mr Chambers wanting to come down to his own place! He is quite definitely coming here on the 8th for three weeks and I suppose it's really very decent of him to let me stay on alone this week. I hoped Mother would come down for a couple of nights but she says she can't leave Charles.

Suzanne writes that she is going back to Foxley Lodge. She never did get on with her parents and now her father has asked her to leave. I believe the glass has been put back in two rooms and they are going to patch up the plaster in her dining-room. But I think she is wrong to do so. I could have found her rooms here a month ago but she declined. If I come back here, to Golf Cottage, it would be too risky to get her to share as we may be turfed out without notice and she is not very mobile, what with Mike and all his impedimenta.

Rocket fell near Uncle Bernard's. Did I tell you they had another doodlebug recently which blew out their windows again and killed three neighbours? They had been to the theatre with them two nights before and Aunt says her morale is now completely gone. So, even if the Roberts weren't in our flat I wouldn't think of going back yet. Looks like being many more months of V-bombs yet.

I don't know how I'm going to stuff into my suitcases all the things I've accumulated since we came. I shall have to take shoes to be mended and clothes to be cleaned to pack it all in. Oliver's toys since Xmas have grown tenfold. I have sold my bike to Betty as there is no chance of using it, and it will be useful to her in Exeter.

Last night I was absorbed in patching a sheet Oliver had put his foot through when I suddenly realised it was nearly midnight. Whereupon I resolved to celebrate for the first time for many years and accordingly poured out a stiff gin from the bottom of the first half bottle and downed it to the accompaniment of many mixed sentiments. It's certainly been a chaotic year for the inmates of Foxley Lodge and the new year promises to be as hectic.

Here's a funny coincidence. Today I went into the village wool shop where there's an assistant with a Scots accent which sticks out a mile among the soft Devon voices. I asked her which part she came from and she answered "Stirling". I simply had to tell her the Ochhills were not covered in snow, at which she blushed delightedly.

Thanks for the paper dart which was what was wanted. But I regret that Oliver took it out and chucked it over the cliff before I had studied its form. The latest game is building houses with Lotts bricks and then sending a doodlebug, complete with siren before and after to knock the roof off.

Time to stop and get on with the mending. What happened to the red pyjamas, which caused you to write pages thereupon? Did your girlfriend mend them for you? Or didn't you trust me with them after all?

Well, darling, let's hope 1945 sees the end of it all and maybe we'll get back where we started from.

Love

Y.

The Lotts Bricks were probably a Christmas present from Clem. In the days before Lego, they were a popular toy construction kit consisting of little bricks made from artificial stone which could be fitted together to build a suburban house and garden, with add-ons, such as a church, hay barn and bus station. The set was advertised under the slogan 'Keep him [sic] Happy (& Quiet)', and promised 'endless fun... British made'.

A week later. Yvonne sits in a wooden shelter on the esplanade which, although the weather is chilly, protects her from enough of the onshore breeze to allow her to be comfortable. She's trying to read the war news in *The Sunday Times,* but the pages flap and flutter annoyingly. A pile of newspapers is on the seat beside her, weighted down by a pebble.

She hears a crash of falling stones and looks up. Oliver is sitting on the beach on the other side of the path. He is separating the pebbles into piles: those he can fit into the palm of his hand, those he can make a fist around and those which are too big for his hand to hold. Once he has sufficient pebbles, he builds each pile into a tower until they collapse. He looks at the wreckage thoughtfully and starts building again.

An old man with a dog walks past followed by a smartly dressed elderly couple on their way to church. Away to her right, two young men in uniform have wheeled out a rickety bath-chair filled with rugs under which an elderly person has been submerged. Only a hand is visible, tremulously tracing the chair's wicker arms. The men point at the vast grey sea and sky and talk quietly together. There is no sound from the chair.

Yvonne watches them for several minutes. Her fingertips sense the thick wickerwork, reminding her of a similar chair a long time ago, also parked on a sea front. When she was about nine years old she was told she had something called spinal TB. Accompanied by her mother, she was driven in a large, dark car to a large, dark house in a place called Broadstairs. Informed she would be staying there several months for the 'sea air', she was bundled into a wheelchair and told to say goodbye to her Mummy. And there she stayed, in the wheelchair, staring at the sea, to 'convalesce'. She was allowed to write only one letter home a week, which the proprietors insisted on checking before it was posted. Broadstairs was where she learned the meaning of the word 'homesick'.

Yvonne feels a sudden chill, as if she were lying again at night in the sad, quiet dormitory full of sickly children, listening out for a sound that scared her: the shuffling steps of a vicious old woman who used to creep into the room at night in her bedroom slippers and mock any patient who was still awake. Later, when Yvonne was home again, she told her mother how unhappy she had been, Horrified, Dorothy said that had she known about the place she would have brought her back immediately. But of course by then it was too late.

That evening she writes again to Clem.

At 17 Victoria Place, Budleigh Salterton

Sunday 7.1.45.

My dear darling,

Your letter Saturday caught me just before we left, but the turkey didn't. I am going up there [to Golf Cottage] tomorrow morning to help Betty get the house ready for the London party and if it doesn't turn up before we finish I will make enquiries at the Post Office and see if it can be brought here directly. But what a pity you won't be here to enjoy it too.

You don't say what size it is but, if it is big enough, I think I'd better let Betty and Dudley have half as we ate theirs all over Xmas and they left us the carcass to scrape when they departed. If there isn't time to get hold of them perhaps Joy could cook it and we'd have a party in her cottage. Anyway, thanks tremendously darling for sending it. I only hope it won't be off by the time I see it!

Please don't be offended if I tell you that I hope to goodness you won't get leave for three weeks. If you have any option please exercise it and fix your leave not before the 29th January. You see, I've got to stay here until then and the idea of us all cooped up in this little room, exactly 10ft square and filled with furniture, makes me awfully miserable. I'm sure we'd all get on each other's nerves and there's nothing you could call homelike about the place. The two beds are equally frightful—I hardly slept last night with a spiral spring sticking up through the thin but lumpy mattress. You can't see at all in the bathroom or bedroom because the lights are heavily shrouded in black material and there's an old lady just across the passage with a nice, continual consumptive croak. Baths, by the way, are 4d extra but lavatory paper, it was stressed, was included. At least the place is clean and smells of soap and not cabbages, and the landlady is quite impersonal, thank goodness, but it makes me uneasy to think of having to pay so much for such miserable accommodation.

I think I can just last out three weeks with the knowledge that we can return to Golf Cottage (although even that isn't certain), even that at 3 guineas weekly would be worth it, and if I can get it for three months I shall easily find someone to share the cost and expenses. All the hotels here are full for some time, packed with old couples who don't move until they die, in fact the whole of Devon is stiff with them. I tried what I thought were two of the more modest kind, but even if they had had rooms they would have charged us seven guineas each and three guineas for Oliver.

If we don't succeed in getting the cottage back I can't think what we'd better do. Even rooms like these are beyond our means and I'm so used to doing the cooking, housework, etc., I'm just not geared for sitting about and being waited on. In fact, that's what's got me down after only one day. I looked at the clock this morning after breakfast. 9.30 and 3½ hours to fill until lunch. We walked along the front and I read six Sunday papers in a shelter. All very depressing.

Roosevelt thinks the war <u>may</u> be over by the end of this year. When I came down here after the bomb I reckoned on being a refugee for about six months, a whole year moving around in other people's houses is a gloomy prospect. But I'm not taking Oliver back to Purley, the people in London are having a very sticky time. More V bombs than ever. Mother heard five explosions in one night, and even your mother wrote that she'd heard three in Merstham [Surrey] in one day.

What a dreary letter for you. Administer the kick in the pants if you like, but surely I can be a bit war weary, at any rate just to you, at times? I should be saying all this to you if you were here, and you'd give me your usual pep talk and things would look brighter.

So, I will stop my meanderings until the atmosphere is more cheerful. But oh how I long for home, especially for your leave.

Y.

P.S. Did you like the photo? You didn't mention it.

Standing outside Victoria Place today, it is surprising Yvonne was so critical of this attractive, cottage-style semi, with its ornamental shutters and little forecourt garden, so conveniently placed between the High Street and the sea. To her, accustomed to the spaciousness of Foxley Lodge and Golf Cottage, it probably did feel like a come-down, especially as she was obliged to pay so much for the rooms. But anyone from a less comfortable background would have been pleased to have lodged there.

It is becoming apparent that V2s are landing further and further away from central London in the direction of Kent and Essex. The MP for Ilford, the borough most under fire, is reported as saying 'If Whitehall were in Essex these attacks would cease.'[136]

MI5 are quietly pleased their deception plan is working well. Ronald Wingate, deputy head of the department co-ordinating military deception, decides to reinforce it. He will plant a question in the House of Commons, the reply to which will elicit the 'information' that a strict news blackout prevents reports of V2s which have landed in central London. General Ismay, Churchill's chief military assistant, gets wind of the idea. He asks Roger Hollis, Head of MI5, what is going on, and Hollis describes the deception plan. In November the previous year, the Twenty Committee noted that the majority of V2s thus far were falling short to the east of the capital, and agreed that it would be left to the double agents to send bare information to their handlers and confirm from decrypted messages that they are being believed. But they don't want to repeat the tortuous exercise of seeking a mandate for their actions. Hollis tells Ismay that 'it would lead to incalculable difficulties if it were to become known that such deception had been the cause of shifting the damage from one part of London to another.' Ismay replies 'We got our fingers badly burnt last time by bringing ministers into this business. I for one do not wish to risk doing so again.'[137] So they agree to keep quiet this time and the V2 deception carries on without official backing. Wingate's question isn't raised in Parliament. However, the discussion has unearthed what is going on and none of them will bear sole responsibility for the consequences.

In early February, Yvonne and Oliver return to Golf Cottage and Clem spends a week's leave with them there, his first since last autumn. He returns to Scotland on February 21st, joining a Holding Brigade stationed at Annan on the Solway Firth. Three days later, Yvonne writes to him.

Golf Cottage, B.S. 24.2.45.

Dearest C.,

So glad to get your cards and to know that your worse fears, at any rate, haven't been realized. In fact, it seems that you are about as well off with a new environment for a mental tonic. I only hope the new C.O. isn't a Blimp[138] and that the rest of the bunch are no worse than usual.

Two days of mist after you left, but then the balmy spring returned. Warm enough to have all the windows wide and not to light the fire until teatime. And how long the days are getting. The sun was just disappearing behind the golf course tonight after I had bedded Oliver. No need for a nightlight with the door left open. This morning I did some light gardening as it was too nice to stay indoors and I couldn't leave the dinner cooking for a walk. Not supposed to touch the garden but don't suppose Mrs Stickley will object to my tidying the flower beds.

Oh dear, just as I was feeling happily settled for a while and looking forward to spring and summer, the future has become precarious again. Mr Stickley has died after all. I learned the news yesterday by being handed a wreath at the front door in error, and then at lunch saw the funeral cortège slowly driving down the slope. I don't suppose we will be turfed out at once, but it looks like goodbye to any idea of having the place to myself for six months. At best I hope to be able to have a couple of rooms here when Mrs S. wants to come back, but that idea may not be any good now as her son in the RAF was posted compassionately to Exmouth and now lives out with her.

Anyway, it is no good worrying in advance. I shall have to wait for her to act and I shall suggest sharing if she doesn't. But I really didn't think he would succumb so soon. Of course it is the proverbial happy release for him.

Funny, I was dozing against the sea wall on Tuesday while Oliver was collecting flat stones and suddenly it came to me how happy I was, more so than I'd been for years and perhaps likely to be for years to come. And then I thought, it's too good to last, it's asking for a disappointment! Herr S. Pants [Soggy Pants] is in good form and much appreciated your card of the ship today. Now you have left your mark on Budleigh he quotes you, what you said, what you did at such-and-such a spot. I was awfully bucked that you took him out for walks alone and he's already mapped out a programme for your next appearance.

Are you messing en masse or eating alone? I could send you up some apples if you like. They are about finished but I think I could save some of the best. It occurred to me that perhaps cider, if you can get it, would satisfy your unrequited craving for fruit. You've certainly started me on the habit. Oliver has just discovered raisins and prefers a handful to a sweet, for the moment.

Fire bubbling away merrily, wireless working much better and now to my toast and coffee. 11 pm.

Much love, Y.

After the anxiety and disruption of the past months, Yvonne's self-confidence is restored and she is contented. Budleigh has worked its magic.

The following week, Yvonne receives an unusual and touching letter. It's from her grandfather, G.F. Brown. Our previous sight of him was as a stern Victorian in a photo at Foxley Lodge and as an elderly man in a private hotel in Croydon, distressed by a broken window. Now we learn he is living in to Exmouth. He has probably been moved there as a result of Yvonne contacting her Uncle Bernard and possibly with the assistance of her Uncle Dudley. Grandpa has celebrated his 91st birthday. It seems that Yvonne and Oliver have visited him, perhaps to reassure Dorothy, who would have wanted to know that her father was comfortably settled.

62 Victoria Road, Exmouth

Saturday 3rd March 1945

My dear Yvonne,

I am very glad to hear from you again. Thank you very much for your letter and your kind invitation. But you have entertained me lavishly already and I think it is up to me to do the next. I should like to see the place where you live, and especially as you may possibly have to give it up, but since my last birthday on the 19th Feb I feel it is more incumbent than ever not to overtire my remaining strength.

I have a slight cold at present and have today paid a visit to the chemist. He has given me some jujubes to suck called 'Meggezones' of which the lid of the box bears the inscription 'Made and guaranteed by Meggeson and Co Ltd, famous since 1796'. It reminds me that when I was a very small boy my grandmother used to send me to Meggesons in Cannon Street in the City of London with a written order for medicine for her.

I am alone now, 5 minutes to 8 pm, in the dining and sitting rooms of this boarding house, of which I am indeed the only guest, so things are not very cheerful. I have not heard from your mother for a long time, but I know she is very troubled with the difficulty of feeding herself and husband, getting coals and no place to store them in.

If you have to move I hope you will come nearer here. I often go to that hill where we parted and imagine I see you and your little boy climbing up it for the bus to the shops.

Good night my one and only,

G.F. Brown

This touching letter suggests that Grandpa wasn't at all the stern paterfamilias he appeared to be in the photo. It also gives us a tiny glimpse into mid-Victorian London, because his boyhood memory of going to the chemist's shop must date from the late 1850s. At this time, his widowed grandmother, born in 1798, lived with his parents at their cheesemonger's shop in Queen Street, by Southwark Bridge. So this little story encompasses five generations of the family.

March 3rd, the date of Grandpa's letter, is also Clem's 40th birthday. And the date of the first of two significant tragedies.

The first is a bombing raid that goes terribly wrong. The Waffen SS has taken over V-weapon operations and are launching both from a wooded area near The Hague called Haagse Bos, aiming them at Antwerp—which, since the Allies captured it at the end of 1944, has been crucial for supplying their troops—as well as at London.[139]Herbert Morrison has been pleading with the Chiefs of Staff for the wood to be bombed to finish off the V-weapons, but his request has been turned down on the grounds that it would divert '1500 Lancaster sorties to counter small scale rocket attacks whose results have no military significance.'[140]

It must have taken some persuasion, but eventually, a mission is agreed and on March 3rd it sets off. It is a catastrophe. The RAF misses the target and instead hits a densely populated area called Bezuidenhout, igniting an intense fire in which over 500 civilians are killed. Buildings are flattened and 20,000 people made homeless. Churchill criticises the RAF for claiming the raid a success. The Chiefs of Staff blame RAF officers for the error. In fact, the mistake seems to have been caused by the wrong coordinates being given to the pilots who, on a foggy night, were unable to see the ground from the air.[141] Leaflets of regret are dropped over the city. The disaster went unreported in Britain.

The second tragedy occurs on the morning of March 8th, when a V2 hits the City of London near Smithfield Market. The Victorian buildings on its west side are destroyed, collapsing first into a deep crater and then further down onto an underground railway. Shoppers, some of whom have been queuing because a consignment of rabbit meat has just arrived, and market workers are crushed in the fall. Some 110 people are killed, including three Air Raid Wardens and a three-year-old child.

Margaret Cotton, an American woman living in London, writes in her diary:

> The act of destruction and death took a few seconds.
>
> The rescue of the victims took a few days.
>
> The billeting of the homeless took a few weeks.
>
> The healing of the injured will take an indefinite time.
>
> The clearing of the bombed and burned site will take some months.
>
> The rebuilding will take years.
>
> The dead are dead.[142]

The following day, Yvonne, who knows nothing of either disaster, writes to Clem enclosing a sheet of scribbles.

Golf Cottage

9.3.45.

Dearest C.,

Sorry to hear of the smelly sheets. They are probably washed with cheap soap. You haven't told me where you feed, or whether you have to make polite conversation or are able to keep your nose in a book.

How long do you give it now? I was listening yesterday evening when the programme was interrupted to give the flash of the Rhine crossing, something I thought would be planned for midsummer. They must be in a chaotic state to allow that to happen. I bet someone is getting it in the pants for not blowing up the bridge properly. Crack on the ITMA programme, "Hitler's name now stinks in Germany because of the Oder-Cologne".

Our day in Sidmouth last Saturday was a great success. Very hot and clear. After lunch in a fly-blown cafe we all climbed the "mountain" on the farther side, passing through numerous fields and then up a narrow zig-zag path until the town lay far below and we could see back to Budleigh. A pile of fifty clean, real bricks occupied the boys while Joy and Joan and I lay on the ground and dozed. It is nearly always warm enough for half an hour on the beach in the morning after shopping. Most of the boats have been repainted and you can buy live lobsters for a shilling. Joy bought one today but it immediately got its claws round poor Chris's little finger and nearly tore the nail off.

Not having seen or heard from Mrs Stickley yet, I am going to broach the subject myself this weekend as I can't go on indefinitely like this, financially speaking. I am tempted to do so though I love it on my own and, contrary to expectations, never feel a bit lonely.

Suzanne has got a break in that Rupert applied for a posting south and has been moved to Bushey Park, Kingston, which means he can get to [her] for the weekend. I feel inclined to demand a similar effort from you but I know what the answer would be, "I'm in the army, not the RAF".

Joy is going up to town for a couple of weeks on the 28th and I am having Peter here for that time. Only too pleased to be able to help her, I was afraid I should be landed with her flea-ridden spaniel but Joan has volunteered to look after her.

Mother and Charles want to come down this way on May 4th for ten days, maybe at Sidmouth. Rosemullion is full and they don't want the Rolle [hotels] as one of Charles's business enemies resides there!

Oliver has found a new pal, Tony, aged four, from the large house opposite. He isn't a bad child but inclined to be spiteful, he chucked Oliver's spade and tins in the hedge just to annoy. His granny "doesn't know" me, not that I care! Spurred on by your enquiry he tried several times to climb the gate in Dark Lane, but so far just can't manage the pivot manoeuvre. He informed me today that you call me "that woman". I waited breathlessly hoping it would be something more endearing.

Have you had your grapefruit yet? My first half today, really the ideal way to start a breakfast. Forgotten how good they tasted. And Teddy Tail [comic strip] is back in the Mail, the war must be over!

Reading "Evenings in Albany" by Clifford Bax. More than a flavour of George Moore.

Love,

Y.

Another letter follows on March 20th, the day after Oliver's fourth birthday.

Monday

Darling,

Lovely surprise parcel from you this afternoon. The jigsaw is just about his level, not too difficult. We did it twice this evening after the party and he got several bits together by himself. The plasticine, I'm afraid, I shall only let him have when I'm there to watch, I have enough of it already trodden into the carpet at home. Such a lot of chocolate too. Hope you don't hanker after it too much, Oliver does appreciate it.

What a day! The weather let us down well and truly. Buckets of rain steadily all day and a terrific wind. Thought the party would be a flop and no-one would turn up, however they all did eventually, soaked to the skin, having tried in vain for a car. Blind man's buff, hunt the ashtray and wheelbarrow races. Enormous tea, Oliver blew out the candles in one go. I made him a fruitcake as he specially asked for it, the passion for raisins still high.

Don't see much of Oliver these days. He is out on the course with Tony all the time. Lost him for hours yesterday and eventually ran him to earth playing on a broken seat by the cliff along a little path he said you had taken him. Keep threatening him I shall be awfully cross if he falls over the edge.

Had to visit the dentist again this week. Turned out to be a new man living on the spot. Further conversation unearthed the fact that he had been bombed out of the Crystal Palace and knew several of Father's contemporaries. He told me I should eat plenty of oranges and drink a pint of milk a day. Very funny. But I got away with only one more filling in the offing.

Oliver is growing in all directions. Nothing fits. Come to think of it, I'm putting on inches around the waist myself, but I'm not so pleased about that.

I think a salmon would be an extremely welcome addition to the bill of fare, but I haven't the slightest idea whether it would weather the journey. Can't you ask one of the other blokes if they've attempted it?

Don't think we've ever thanked you for the numerous cards. Oliver is always very excited over them. They stand on the mantelpiece for a couple of days and then he cuts them out.

Your last letter only a covering note. So you owe me two.
There isn't much to write about nowadays, is there?

Y

A three-month gap in the correspondence follows. There doesn't seem
to be a particular reason for this, perhaps Yvonne hadn't much to write
about or they were able to telephone each other.

The last major V2 tragedy occurs at the end of March, when three
tenement blocks in Stepney are hit, killing 134 residents including
30 children. It is the day before Passover and 120 of the dead are
Jewish. Later the same day, the last V2 to be fired at England lands in
Orpington, Kent, behind the Commodore cinema, blasting the centre
of the town to pieces. Ivy Millichamp becomes the last Briton to be
killed by a V-weapon. She had gone into her kitchen to boil a kettle.

The V2 launch sites are overrun by Allied troops and the RAF bombs
the town of Nordhausen close to where the V-weapon factory is
situated. Some 8,500 people are killed, including 1,500 sick prisoners.
The Germans herd over a thousand slave labourers into a barn at
Gardelegen, douse them with petrol and gun them down. A train
carrying rocket parts, scheduled for destruction by the Nazis to prevent
them falling into Allied hands, is 'rescued' by American troops, who
also pick up von Braun and his team. The rocket mastermind has got
what he wanted, but is later disappointed to discover the Americans
are more interested using his technology for military purposes rather
than moonshots. Meanwhile, Berlin has been completely encircled by
the Red Army.

On April 26th, responding to a planted question in the House of
Commons, Churchill announces that the rocket campaign has ended.
Three days later, the last V1s arrive: one at Waltham Cross and one
at Chislehurst, with the final hurrah being one that lands on a sewage

farm in Datchworth, Hertfordshire; an inglorious end to the 'miracle' weapons.

In terms of statistics, the entire V-weapons campaign in Britain caused 11,855 deaths and over 30,000 civilian casualties. They destroyed 107,000 homes, with over a million and a half more left in need of repair.[143] Somewhere between nine and ten thousand V1s were launched at London:[144] 2,419 reached their target, killing 6,184 people and injuring 17,981;[145] 142 struck Croydon, killing 211 people and injuring nearly 2,000. [146] Coulsdon and Purley, with 57 flying bombs, was the eleventh worst-hit borough. In fact, 14.5% of all British civilian deaths in the second world war were caused by V1s. As for the V2s, 1,402 were fired at England, of which 1,358 reached the London area. An estimated 2,754 civilians were killed and some 6,500 injured. Ilford (35) and Woolwich (33) were the boroughs worst hit.[147]

However, it's worth putting these figures into context. Although it may have been of little comfort to those in the south east of Britain, Churchill was right to say that German civilians were suffering much worse. According to historian David Edgerton,

> 'By the end of the war, Bomber Command could, in twenty-four hours, drop more bombs on Germany than the tonnage launched against Britain by all the flying-bomb attacks of 1944, and more too than was dropped on London during all the months of the Blitz. The British killed somewhere between 150,000 and 300,00 German civilians by bombing—the figures are highly uncertain—three to six times as many as British civilians killed by the Germans.'[148]

Half of Germany's housing stock was lost in the war and 73 million people were made homeless.[149]

From the global perspective, UK civilian deaths in the Second World War numbered a mere 0.13%[150]of the world total. The corresponding figures for Germany were somewhere between 1.5 and 3 million, in Poland around 5.5 million and in the Soviet Union 4.5 to 10 million.[151] Worldwide, approximately 50 million civilians were killed with a further 19–28 million dying from disease and famine[152].

What about the deception plan? In south London, conspiracy theories circulated long after the end of the war. One suggested that someone 'high up' in government had fixed it for Croydon to be sacrificed because he feared that the East End Londoners would rise up in arms if they had to endure anything like the Blitz again.

In 1964, when the War Cabinet papers from twenty years before were made public, historian David Irving published a book called *The Mare's Nest* accompanied by an article in the *Sunday Telegraph*. These revealed the extent of the V1 deception plan and the discussions that took place about its authorisation.[153] Those who, like Yvonne, had lived through that 'doodlebug summer' were shocked but not entirely surprised to discover the truth: that the government had accepted that Croydon would be put in the firing line so that lives in more densely populated boroughs would be spared.

But since then further evidence has come to light. In the 1978 historian Richard Anthony Young claimed that, having read Garbo's initial reports, the Germans gradually shortened their aim, even when messages from their (double) agents conflicted with the more accurate data they received from bombs with wireless transmitters.[154] On the other hand, in 1990, Michael Howard confirmed from German army records that the unit responsible for the despatch of flying bombs, 'at no point thought it necessary to adjust its aim'. Instead, they relied on the test firing data for their aim, together with the wireless transmission from the Tower Bridge bomb and reports from an imaginative agent in Madrid, apparently outside British control, who told them London was being pummelled to smithereens. The result was that V1s continued to fall short of their target.[155]

After all, accurate aiming wasn't essential for a terror weapon. As long as the flying bombs fell somewhere in the London area they were considered to be successful. As H.E. Bates put it, 'If you aim at the docks and hit the Guildhall, if you aim at Victoria Station and hit the Tower of London, if you aim at Battersea Power Station and hit the house where Dickens wrote *Pickwick Papers*, it does not really matter.... You never miss.'[156]

So it seems the deception plan had less effect than MI5 thought even though, when one of its architects died in 1982, his obituary in *The Times* included the words, 'Many citizens of London who survived the V-bombs ... owe their lives to Charles Cholmondeley.'[157] Instead, the real success of the deception plan was that, by protecting the double agents' credibility, Fortitudes South and North remained plausible far longer than had been anticipated, allowing Allied troops to fight on in Normandy for nearly two months without having to face the thousands of Nazi troops kept in Calais and Denmark. Perhaps the Chiefs of Staff would have been more willing to endorse the plan if they had they had known this.

As for the impact of the V-weapons on British morale, after the first few terrifying weeks civilians became frustrated at their continuance but for the most part were wearily stoic. By 1945 many would have agreed with London diarist, Vere Hodgson, who wrote that it was 'only the spring' that was keeping her going.[158] They were fortunate in that an Allied bombing raid at the end of 1943 had delayed the V-weapon programme by several months and bought valuable time; had the V1s and V2s arrived sooner, for example before D-Day, or in greater numbers, the consequences could have been disastrous for the Allies.

May 3rd: Yvonne's 34th birthday. She was probably able to mark it with greater cheer than in the previous six years, but nothing survives to tell us if she did, apart from a little book called *Wild Flowers of the Wayside and Woodland* on the flyleaf of which Yvonne has written 'Budleigh Salterton, 3rd May 1945, from Mother', so perhaps Dorothy and Charles were there to celebrate the day with her.

May 8th is declared VE Day: Victory in Europe. The Soviet Army occupies Berlin, Hitler has committed suicide and the war is over. In London, Churchill and the Royal Family make public appearances and huge crowds light bonfires in Trafalgar Square and jump into the fountains. They dance along the Mall, where a 23-year-old soldier called Humphrey Lyttleton entertains them on a trumpet. As darkness falls, searchlights pick out chaotic congas winding around the streets and in the City, the iconic facade of St Paul's Cathedral is lit up by searchlights.

Budleigh celebrates too. Church bells ring, the town is draped with flags and a brass band plays on the football pitch. Yvonne and Oliver attend a service of thanksgiving in St Peter's Church. The powerful and uplifting hymns, *Now Thank We All Our God, All People That On Earth Do Dwell* and *Abide With Me* bookend prayers commending 'to God's keeping all who have fallen in battle and all who have died in attacks on their country.' Perhaps Yvonne remembers, among others, her youthful admirer. They sing the National Anthem and take a collection for the Christian reconstruction of a liberated Europe.

How Yvonne spends the rest of the day isn't known, but she had plenty of options because everyone lets their hair down, Budleigh-style. In the big houses, bottles of Champagne are brought out of storage, while in the garden of her home in Cliff Terrace, a Mrs Pantoll serves afternoon teas. As evening approaches, everyone celebrates the end of the blackout by switching on their gas lights and leaving all the curtains open so that streets and gardens are ablaze. Air-raid sirens sound a final, victorious All Clear. There's a dance in the Public Hall. American soldiers tear around town in jeeps, whooping and blaring horns.[159] At the Salterton Arms, a piano is wheeled out to the street and a crowd gathers round it to sing *Roll Out the Barrel, We'll Meet Again* and *Shine on Victory Moon.* Those more inclined to quiet reflection gather on the beach to contemplate the place in history of this momentous day and watch the waves roll indifferently onto the pebbled shore.[160]

Nearly two months later, at the end of June, Yvonne writes to the newly promoted, 'Major C.L. Shaw', now based at the Churchill Barracks in Ayr, the Royal Scots Fusiliers depot. It seems Clem has noticed a shortage of letters from her.

Golf Cottage, Friday 29.6.45.

Dearest C.,

I am sorry. Here's a shot at making amends, though there's no body in it. We're still waiting for the summer, taking tea down to the beach and generally having to eat it in the shelter out of the rain. Infuriating, because the long evenings are generally fine, and I am now beginning to find them a bit too long on my own with nothing much to do and no one to do it with!

I actually went to the pictures last night, a poor show, but anyway won't even do that again as when I got back I found Oliver still awake at 10.30 having a quiet cry. Goodness knows how long he'd been at it, he was almost asleep when I left.

Very glad you are enjoying army life at last but I just don't believe your bit about playing squash for 5½ hours. As I remember it about forty minutes fast play was enough for anyone. I know I had to have a couple of beers after it, and a shower, before I could utter a complete sentence. Still, maybe you included beer drinking in the sum total?

Had a very pleasant 2½ days with mother last weekend, the first time I've had her on her own for some time since she remarried. We only pottered but the time simply flew. Now I'm planning mental menus for Uncle and Aunt next weekend. The fruit season is in full swing here and I wish I could send you up some strawberries and raspberries, but I remember trying the latter on you once with dire results. It will be tough if Oliver is to go through life allergic to them. I now make him have them on bread and butter. He gets a great kick out of the ice cream, which seems frightful muck to me, must be just frozen dried milk. Still, it's something to buy without coupons.

We went to the christening of Tony's young brother this week and afterwards back for a cocktail party. The first part was exceedingly dull but after all the old ladies had been given tea and departed the drinks and more interesting people appeared and I really enjoyed it immensely. I rolled back here at eight ready to go on anywhere but, anticlimax, had to put Oliver to bed and sober up on coffee. I should leap at the chance of dressing up. I feel a bit sad to think I've never been to a single service "do" with you. The next evening we went in a party up to the marine camp to hear Solomon [classical pianist] give a concert.

Are you still not going to vote? I've changed from a lukewarm Conservative to an absolute partisan. Reading that the socialists ended up at Blackpool with the Russian anthem quite finished me. Labour canvassing seems quite non-existent here, in fact I haven't seen a single poster or leaflet about their member.

By the way, according to Eileen Holmes[161] the regular army is masonic-ridden. I've never heard that before. Do you agree?

After much scratching and heavy thought, the only bright remark worth passing on came out yesterday when Oliver insisted that he had seen the circus ring master coming out of church. It was, of course, a seedy-looking undertaker's assistant. The circus is tomorrow. Rather a bore but can't disappoint him. It looks from the poster exactly the same as the one last month. We are going en masse in the cheapest seats with lots of buns.[162]

By the way, I think we are all right for August here but I am almost sure that the cottage is let to Mr Chambers for September. I know he has written to Mrs Stickley for it then, Betty told me so. I didn't think you would want to stay on but, if you do, let me know at once and I will see if he will postpone until October, he originally wanted to come then. From the papers Group 11 will be out at least by August 11th, so you ought to have most of August here anyway. You will let me know directly you know the date, won't you?

This place is full of moths. I really think you ought to look at your clothes before you come down, shake them and stick in some more camphor. You could then bring some shirts and a pair of shorts down too. I read too that besides a full civilian clothing book you will be given 90 extra coupons. Just you wait until I lay my hands on them!

Much love to the B.G.O. [no idea] from the E.L.W. [Ever-Loving Woman]

Another English summer has failed to live up to expectations. More worrying is the episode of Oliver in tears; it seems Yvonne hasn't paid attention to her Mother's letter in the local newspaper all those years before. Surely Yvonne didn't leave him all evening by himself? It wasn't unknown in those days for parents to go out without their children in the evenings, especially if they weren't going far, but Yvonne never leaves Oliver alone like this again.

It was almost certain that she saw the film at the Public Hall in Budleigh, and it may have been *The Life and Death of Colonel Blimp* which was in circulation in the area at the time. If so, it is surprising that she rated what is generally reckoned to be a wartime classic as 'a poor show'.

Churchill calls a General Election with polling to take place in early July. Clem has told Yvonne he isn't going to vote—his political views are closest to the Liberal Party, for whom he worked before the war as a Press Officer. Being a solid middle-class Tory, it isn't surprising Yvonne is outraged by the Labour Party singing the Russian national anthem at their conference. She would have agreed with Sir Herbert Williams' warnings of socialism and, even worse, communism.

In fierce electoral campaign, the Lewisham V1 tragedy plays a part. Herbert Morrison stands for Labour in the Conservative-held constituency; after Croydon and Wandsworth, Lewisham was the borough most hit by flying bombs. Churchill, who strongly dislikes Morrison, insinuates it was the Home Secretary's inefficiency that led to there being no air-raid warning before the doodlebug struck.[163] Morrison replies that, although obviously it was the Germans who were responsible for the bombing, it was Churchill who, at a Civil Defence meeting, had ordered that sirens need not be sounded if only a single V1 was sighted, adding that after the Lewisham bomb, he countermanded the order.[164]

Just before polling day, Churchill visits Lewisham in person. A large crowd takes to the streets to see him and, as the local paper puts it, people 'mad with excitement' surge forward just to touch his hand. He delivers a speech to them in which he takes responsibility for the defence of London but adds of Morrison, 'Of all the colleagues I have lost, he is the one I am least sorry to have seen the last of. I hope Lewisham will throw this intruder out.' Morrison responds in the press that he was entitled to give his side of the story, adding 'His concluding spiteful and petty references to me are unworthy...'[165]

When the results of the election are announced, Morrison wins Lewisham East with 62% of the vote. For some time afterwards, Churchill refuses to speak to him. Other Conservatives who lose their seats are Duncan Sandys in Norwood, another heavily bombed borough, and Sir Herbert Williams, who blames the loss of his seat in South Croydon on the response of his constituents to the Rustington beach trespass, 'because [they] thought it very wrong that their M.P. should have broken the law.'[166] He is unrepentant.

Yvonne's next letter is undated but is written in mid-July.

Golf Cottage, Friday.

Dearest C.,

I believe you are still one up, so this should equalize the score. I'm a pricked balloon, Uncle and Aunt having to cancel their visit at the last moment, Aunt being stricken with lumbago. And everything seems to be going so well, even the weather has come up to scratch and I managed to procure an enormous chicken (now passed on to Tony's family) and lashings of raspberries (now devoured by Oliver and me) and had found a pleasant fourth for some gentle bridge. Now I don't suppose I shall see them until we go home, although they have booked up at the Rolle [Hotel] for ten days in September.

Everyone here is much shaken by yesterday's tragedy when Mrs Cooper, a rich, attractive widow threw herself over the cliffs at the top of Victoria Place. She was killed instantly. Blissfully ignorant, Oliver and I were sitting on the beach a few yards from the spot only a couple of hours later, and oddly enough I wrote a letter to Mother there ending up that, 'Oliver was climbing the cliff and looked like committing suicide'. There you have the germ of a story, surely. She had been at the Rolle for five years and played a daily round of golf and generally had a word with Oliver at the end of it.

Would you mind if I had Jennie down to stay for a week, or maybe two? Joy's aunt is coming down on the 27th and could escort her on the journey and Rupert could fetch her home. I'm asking particularly as I hope and imagine you will be here for some, if not all, of the time. I'd like to do something for the kid and she can't remember her last seaside holiday. Rupert is getting ten days' leave on the 27th, so Suzanne is parking out Michael and they are having a suburban holiday at home going to the flicks and having days in town, aren't some people queer! I had asked her to come too, for the beginning of this month.

Oliver wants me to tell you about his garden. The first flower, a cornflower, should be out in about five days and he intends to send it to you. He has a new thrill, having rides on the motorbike with Mr Harris's son. He and Tony wait for him in the middle of the road about six o clock and the poor man isn't allowed to put it away until they have both been down Sherbrook Hill, seated on the engine.[167]

By the way, we've been asked to a wedding (August 11th) which is to be at Sevenoaks. I will decline the invitation for us (unless you are dying to attend). Shall I sling our surplus set of jug and six tumblers? It was a wedding present and we have never used them.

Just here, Eileen Holmes popped over bearing aloft a cake she promised to make me. We've been jawing over a cuppa and now it's 11pm and my creative urge is at rock bottom. Do write and tell me whether you have made up your mind yet. But, if you have, you will maybe change it!

Y xxxx.

The day before she wrote this letter, the body of Mrs Edith Cooper was found 200 feet below the cliffs. She was 39, the widow of a Captain Charles Cooper of the Devonshire Regiment, and had lived at the Rolle Hotel for four years. At the inquest, her doctor explained that 'she had a complex as to her age and had a dread of getting old.' The Coroner returned a verdict of suicide while the balance of her mind was disturbed, saying she 'seemed to [have] no motive except depression through illness.' Whether this was the actual cause or more was involved we do not know.

Peacetime brings its own challenges. On the evening of Yvonne's letter, the BBC broadcasts a talk by the Secretary of the Marriage Guidance Council entitled 'Coming Home: a Christian view of the problems of home and family life today.' Reuniting families after six years of war was portrayed as the happy-ever-after ending to the war, when 'the boys came back', and for many this was the case. But for others, months if not years of family separation and different experiences had changed people's character and, for some, living together again was going to be difficult if not impossible.

The film *Brief Encounter,* released in the autumn of 1945, captures the kind of relationship that often developed in wartime when strangers were brought together in an air-raid shelter or a British Restaurant, or on a railway station platform cafe. Its romantic story relies on the possibility that anyone, even a nice, sensible middle-class woman, might be tempted to compromise her marriage vows, albeit on this occasion with British restraint and wistful might-have-beens. There is, of course, a happy ending, showing how a spouse might show tact and patience to an erring partner, but in real life these qualities were often in short supply.[168]

The evacuees are heading home now. In Budleigh, a meeting of the Town Council learns that over 200 mothers and children have been billeted there under the government's official scheme (Yvonne and Oliver were unofficial evacuees, of which also there were many in the town). The chairman thanks residents for their generous welcome and says he thought 'most people had been very kind.' However, a Mr Hooker disagrees, saying that 'In once case an old lady had a mother and four children put on her, while a man and his wife with three bedrooms got out of it without any evacuees at all.'[169] As the evacuees make their way home, *The Devon and Exeter Gazette* includes what is probably a fictional conversation in Devonian dialect.

> 'Yesterday I met with ole Ted, as I told 'ee, and he'd then bin to zee they two children off, by train, back to Lunnon. I thought the ole feller would 'ave broke his 'art.
>
> 'Tis like losing my own,' he saith, 'The plaace ab'm bin the zame since they two youngsters has bin there, and now us veels as if us can't spare 'em. They took to callin' us "Mum" an' "Dad", and arter vive years the houze won't zeem right wai'out 'em. All us can do now is to look vore to the time when tey comes down again for their skule hollerdys."[170]

Yvonne's last letter to Clem is sent on July 10th. The envelope contains two dried cornflowers and a single sheet of paper on which is written in pencil 'The first flowers from the garden', underneath which Oliver has proudly printed his name.

In July, a different, musical seed is planted. A young Fleet Air Arm officer and musician appears on the regular radio programme entitled 'Navy Mixture.' It's a variety show with a quiz, songs, comedy and a magician; a magician performing on the radio being as improbable as a ventriloquist. The young officer performs one of his own compositions, a Prelude.[171]

The seed germinates. Twenty years later in a London recording studio, this former officer supervises the recording of a song written and performed by four young men, all of whom were born during the war and one of whom is blessed with the middle name of Winston. The record races to Number One in the pop charts. The man is George Martin, the group is The Beatles and the single is 'A Hard Day's Night', the title song from their first film. In one moment of the movie, a limousine carrying the group swerves round a street corner to reveal a brief glimpse of Whitfield Street. Three years later, when the group chooses images of people they admire for the front cover of their album, *Sgt Pepper's Lonely Hearts Club Band*, Issy Bonn, singer of *Shine on Victory Moon*, is included.

On August 2nd Clem is demobbed from the army, but he has already travelled to Budleigh to join Yvonne and Oliver for a short holiday. Then it is time for them to pack up, say goodbye to the little town and return home. With luck, love and determination, they have seen it through.

But that's not quite the end of the story.

Afterword
1945 to 1973

They never went back, not even for a visit. Seaside holidays were taken in places within easier reach of south London, resorts like Bognor Regis and Bexhill. I suppose Clem and Yvonne might have considered going back to live in Budleigh when he retired but, as things turned out, that possibility never arose.

To begin with, all went well. Clem, Yvonne and Oliver resumed sharing Foxley Lodge with Rupert, Suzanne, Jennie and Michael. There were advantages to this arrangement in the bleak late 1940s: sharing food, fuel, cigarettes—the adults all smoked like chimneys—and company. Rupert set up his dental practice on the ground floor of the house and Clem joined the phalanx of commuters travelling to London, working as press officer for the Brewers' Society; a job found for him, inevitably, by Uncle Bernard. Yvonne and Suzanne cared for the children and ran their households, sharing a 'cleaning woman' and stretching meagre rations to fill hungry tummies.

Later, looking back on it, the children remembered those days as resembling an Enid Blyton story. Jennie captained a gang consisting of Oliver, Michael and two children from next door, an Infamous Five. They even had a dog. Rupert built a tree house for them in the wood, they played croquet and cricket on the lawn. They raced homemade go-karts down Olden Lane past the St Marie bombsite and into Dale Road where, on one occasion Michael struck a lamp-post and knocked out a couple of teeth. Lucky for him, his Dad was a dentist.

In 1946 a letter from Germany arrived at Foxley Lodge addressed to Yvonne. It was from Otto Kozusnicek. He had not forgotten her. He asked whether she had survived the war and under what circumstances.

For his part, he told her he had suffered at the hands of first the Red Army and then the Czechs. In poor health and weak from lack of food, he explained that he had lost everything: his business, his home and all his possessions. His main reason for writing though, was that he hoped she still remembered him and the happy times they had shared. What she must have thought when she read this letter is difficult to imagine; still less how, assuming she replied, she broke the news to him that she was married with a son. But she kept his letter.

As the 1940s ended, Yvonne's health began to deteriorate. It's impossible to say what caused it, there were several possible factors: her childhood illness, years of poor diet, a delayed reaction to the stresses of war and perhaps the strain of adjusting to post-war life with a full-time husband. Of course, her experiences hadn't been as terrible as those endured by so many others during the war: she was never hit by a bomb, imprisoned, beaten or starved; but, ultimately, comparisons are of limited value. As journalist Hugo Rifkind wrote recently about the reporter Fergal Keane, who has witnessed some of the most terrible atrocities of recent conflicts, 'You don't need to earn the right to feel things ... We're people. We hurt. That's all we need to know.'[172] After a couple of weeks in hospital enduring tests and increasingly bizarre diets, she became so hungry and depressed that she discharged herself. Fortunately, something must have happened to improve her health because a year later I was born.

In the early 1950s, Dorothy's husband, Charles, died, leaving her well provided for. She sold the Chelsea flat and bought two houses: one for Rupert and his family in Reigate and another in Purley, divided between a new dental practice for him on the ground floor and a flat on the first for herself.[173] This left Clem, Yvonne, Oliver and the new baby, me, with the run of Foxley Lodge.

So that's where I grew up, in that large, cold, impractical house. Yvonne, my mum, performed the role designed for her by 1950s' convention, that of housewife and mother. She cooked and washed and ironed and shopped with a paid 'help' coming in three mornings a week to clean and polish. In the afternoons, she listened to 'Woman's Hour' on the radio, did the crossword in the *Daily Telegraph*, maintained the large garden and went to tea with her friends or her mother. There were occasional trips to the cinema or, as she called it 'the flicks', lunchtime recitals in Croydon and the occasional theatre performance in London. If this existence bored or frustrated her there is little evidence of it in her letters and diaries. After all, she was living the life she had longed for throughout the war and most of her friends would have said the same.

Budleigh was a memory packaged up and put away in the attic of family history. On the few occasions it was mentioned in conversation, everybody smiled and looked happy, so I grew up thinking it must be some sort of Shangri-La, a magical place possessed of restorative powers where the sea always sparkled, the pebbles on the beach shone brightly and the cliffs glowed red in the setting sun. But when I asked, 'Can we go there?' the answer was always, 'No, it's too far away.'

In Purley, new buildings appeared, replacing the rubble and weed-strewn waste grounds, but the war still hung in the air like the dust around a bombsite. Houses had cracks in the ceilings and patches of plaster missing from their walls. At the bottom of the gardens lurked dank, smelly air-raid shelters that you didn't go into. At mealtimes, the men talked about battle positions and military incompetence and judged any new acquaintances by what they did in the war; the women reminisced about the home front: the ghastly food, the lack of scissors and razor blades. They hoarded bits of string and wrapping paper, insisted their children ate everything on their plates and told them how very lucky they were to be able to buy sweets. When an air-raid siren sounded on a tv programme, Mum would quietly get up and leave the room. 'Why does she do that?' I asked my father. 'I suppose she heard enough of them in the war', he would reply, leaving her alone with her thoughts.

In 1959, Oliver left boarding school and began work as a shipping clerk in the City of London, following his father as a commuter. He spent his evenings practising classical guitar or tinkering with old radios in the attics of Foxley Lodge; or going out with friends and local girls. Everything seemed to be going well until sadly, within a year, there were signs he was seriously ill. Clem and Yvonne were given the terrible news: their son had Hodgkin's lymphoma, which in those days was incurable.

There is a particular form of this disease, the preconditions for which describe Oliver almost perfectly: 'the first or only child of a well-to-do family, have an educated mother, spend childhood in a single-family house with few playmates and have few common childhood infections.'[174] Surgery and treatment were attempted but the disease spread rapidly. Determined not to abandon him, Mum nursed him at home until the end. In May 1961 he died, aged 20. The loss was devastating. War had forged a close bond between mother and son. He had been, as she put it, her 'war work', and she had nurtured him thereafter, only to lose him just as he reached adulthood. After his death, she couldn't face living at Foxley Lodge and was adamant no one else should either, so we moved elsewhere and the house was demolished.

Perhaps, if she had been able to find fulfilling work outside home, she might have found new interests and been able to bear the loss of her son better. But at 50 years old and without work experience for two decades, that was virtually impossible. So Mum tried yoga, vegetarianism, voluntary work, psychiatric help and giving up smoking, none of which helped for long. Clem thought them all nonsense anyway. Buck up, old girl.

Her health collapsed. More hospital stays, more barium meals, X-rays and strange diets. Eventually she was diagnosed with Crohn's disease and various associated conditions, but by that time she was worn out, depressed and emotionally exhausted. In 1965, aged 53, she died. Clem, who had lost both his son and his wife, struggled on, but even after remarrying became an anxious and remorseful man, isolated in grief. In 1973, he died of cancer.

So this book, this attempt to rub the glass and peer into the world before I was born, is also my journey back to my lost family. I've found Yvonne and Oliver sharing their life together, hearing that sinister drone and glancing up at the clouds; and sitting by an upturned boat on a pebbled seashore with her friend, young children and a dog. Clem, though the absent note of the triad, is often in their thoughts, his occasional presence allowing the chord to be struck.

How different was that world from the one I fitted into later on, growing up in the fifties and sixties. Tight budgets, yes, but food more plentiful, sweets in the sweet shop, toys left over from the Infamous Five and the lawn mower stored in what had once been an air raid shelter. I'm glad Mum wrote that she was, 'more than a bit envious and would like to be Suzanne up the road just now. How about it?' even if it was some time before that wish was fulfilled, but above all am very grateful to my father for keeping her letters, allowing me this glimpse into their lives.

We'll turn to the other people mentioned in Yvonne's letters.

Rupert practised dentistry in Purley until retirement, but later developed Alzheimer's Disease and died in the mid-1980s, Suzanne shortly afterwards. Both Jennie and Michael went to live abroad: Jennie to Canada, where she married, had three children and lived in Vancouver until her death in 2019: Michael to France where he married and had two daughters and where, sadly, he suffered from depression and took his own life in the 2000s.

'Grandpa' G.F. Brown, died in Exmouth in 1947, Dorothy in Purley in 1962. Uncle Dudley and Aunt Florrie are untraceable, although their son Peter was last recorded farming in New Zealand in the 1950s; Uncle Bernard and Aunt Doris lived in Chichester until the mid-1970s.

After the war, Joy Richards went abroad with her husband and two boys. In 1957, when her mother died, she was left a tidy sum as 'a single woman,' which suggests that by then she was divorced from her second husband. The following year, she married a farmer called Oliver Muspratt. Mum's diary shows that she didn't attend the wedding, but Joy visited us during that summer. By the early 1960s, they were living abroad in another fishing village, this time on the Spanish Mediterranean coast. She died in 1996.

Out of office, Sir Herbert Williams sold his house in Rustington. Back in the 1930s, he had served as Secretary to Empire Economic Union, a pressure group funded partly by the Canadian Lord Beaverbrook, which lobbied for free trade agreements between the UK and the dominions. During the Second World War, the union was mothballed because its aims conflicted with those of the USA, but as soon as it was over, Williams reformed the group. He opposed America's plan for Britain to form a closer alliance with other European countries because he saw it as a step towards ending the British Empire. In 1948, as Chairman of the Conservative Party, Williams told Beaverbrook after its annual conference that he was 'confident he had killed off any serious agitation inside the party' to form closer ties with Europe. Beaverbrook was delighted and wrote to him. 'Remember the Empire.

You are responsible for seeing that the Conservatives do not sell us down the river more than once a year.'[175]

When constituency boundaries were redrawn for the 1950 general election, Williams was offered the chance to campaign for the new seat of Croydon East, which he won with a majority of 9,000. Four years later, after speaking in an evening debate regarding refurbishments to the House of Commons, he suffered a stroke and died a few days later. In his memoir, *Politics—grave and gay*, Williams refers once to Croydon South and, curiously, only to the flying bombs that fell near his home in Sussex.

When doodlebugs are mentioned, one memory comes back to me: that of a cool, dry Sunday morning in autumn or early winter, possibly in November 1954. Mum is in the kitchen at the back of Foxley Lodge, cooking roast beef and Yorkshire pudding.

I am three years old. My brother, ten years older than me, lanky, dark-haired, is in the hall, asking my father if we can go to 'the bombsite' just up the road. A coat is wrapped around me and buttoned up. Oliver pushes woolly mittens onto my hands. 'Keep your fingers straight', he says. 'There'. He turns to our father, so tall and as distant as a castle. 'Can we? The bombsite?'

'Don't tell your mother.'

We set off up Dale Road. My brother's long legs take him out in front, he's wearing grey trousers and black shoes, and a jacket he calls a blazer.

When we arrive, it is the strangest place I have ever seen. Where a house should have stood between two others is an enormous gap with pieces of twisted metal, chunks of plaster, parts of a wooden door leaning sideways and bits of brick lying about casually or piled in untidy heaps. It's all covered in a soft dust which, as my brother crunches away from me, floats up behind him and fills the air. It makes me cough. Something about this place makes me uncomfortable, although I don't know why, and I sense my father is wondering whether we should have come here after all.

Oliver slips and slithers on the bricks. His shoes are getting dusty. He shouts, 'There's not much here... uh, I think this is a teapot lid, but it's all smashed up'.

'Can I look too?' I ask. My father grabs my hand. It is lost in his huge gloved paw.

'No.'

'But ...'

'It's too dangerous for you.'

This is disappointing. But also a bit of a relief because I realise I do not like the look of these broken things. They are not supposed to look like this.

'Why is it all like this?' I ask, climbing onto a broken brick and balancing on it.

'It's a bombsite...'

'What's a bombsite?'

'It's where a bomb fell a few years ago and blew up a house.'

This is worrying news. I do not like this bomb.

'And will the bomb fall down again?'

'No,' he says, firmly and reassuringly.

My brother shouts, and clambers towards us, holding something in his hand.

'Dad! Look, is this a bit of the doodlebug?'

He gives it to my father, who looks at it thoughtfully. The brick I am standing on is wobbly, but I manage to space out my feet so I can tilt it up and down, like a tiny see-saw.

My father inspects the lump of metal.

'Don't think so,' he says, 'looks like... no, I don't know what it is...'

'I'll take it into school tomorrow.' He slides it into his blazer pocket.

'Daddy! Woliver! Look! I made a see-saw!' I wobble on my brick.

'Come on', says my father, 'let's go up the hill to the park.'

I look down. Now it seems the distance between my unstable brick and the ground is ever so big. I am afraid to jump off. I hold up my arms in an appeal for assistance. My father is staring at the heaps of rubble.

'Remember this,' he says.

'Why?'

'Because it's the last time you'll see it. They're going to build houses here.'

I smile at my daddy. I will remember.

He takes one arm, my brother the other, and I am swung up so high into the air that all I can see above me is the wide, safe sky.

Bibliography

Yvonne Shaw's letters are held at the Imperial War Museum: The private papers of Mrs Y.M.L. Shaw https://www.iwm.org.uk/collections/item/object/1030003071.

I would not have been able to write this book without reference to Norman Longmate's *The Doodlebugs*, which contains the full story of the V1s and accounts from those who lived through their attacks, and the more recent *Target London* by Christy Campbell, which brings the history of both V-weapons up to date and includes information about the deception plans and material drawn from secret decrypts.

General

Arthur, Max (2004) *Forgotten Voices of the Second World War*, Ebury Press, London.

BBC Programme Index https://genome.ch.bbc.co.uk/

British Newspaper Archive https://www.britishnewspaperarchive.co.uk/

Chisholm, Anne and Davie & Michael (1992) *Beaverbrook: A Life*, Hutchinson, London.

Collingham, Lizzie (2011) *The Taste of War: World War Two and the Battle for Food*, Allen Lane, London.

Donoghue, Bernard and Jones, G.W. (1973) *Herbert Morrison*, Weidenfeld and Nicholson, London.

Edgerton, David (2010) *Britain's War Machine: Weapons, Resources and Experts in the Second World War*, Allen Lane, London.

Euden, Tony (2007) *The Children's Convalescent Homes of Broadstairs,* Michaels Bookshop, Ramsgate, Kent.

Gardiner, Juliet (2004) *Wartime: Britain 1939–1945,* Headline Book Publishing, London.

Hermiston, Roger (2016) *All Behind You, Winston: Churchill's Great Coalition 1940–45,* Aurum Press Ltd., London.

Hodgson, Vere (1999) *Few Eggs and No Oranges: The Diaries of Vere Hodgson 1940–45,* Persephone Books, London.

Holland, James & Murray Al, (2022) 'Churchill's War Room', *We have ways of making you talk, podcast* 4 May 2022, available at https://player.fm/series/we-have-ways-of-making-you-talk/churchills-war-room

Huber, Florian (2020) *Promise Me You'll Shoot Yourself: The Downfall of Ordinary Germans, 1945,* Penguin Books, London. (Translated by Imogen Taylor)

Jenkins, Roy (2001) *Churchill: a biography,* MacMillan, London.

Lewisohn, Mark (2013) *All These Years, Volume 1: Tune In,* Little, Brown, London.

Met Office Digital Library https://digital.nmla.metoffice.gov.uk/

Minns, Raynes (1980) *Bombers and Mash: the Domestic Front 1939–45,* Virago Ltd., London.

Morrison of Lambeth (1960) *Herbert Morrison, an autobiography,* Odhams, London.

Overy, Richard (2020) *The Dangers of the Blitz Spirit,* History Extra.

https://www.historyextra.com/period/second-world-war/the-dangers-of-the-blitz-spirit/

Sangster, Andrew ((2021) *Alan Brooke: Churchill's right-hand man,* Casemate Publishers, Oxford.

Schneer, Jonathan (2015) *Ministers at war: Winston Churchill and his war cabinet,* Oneworld Publications, London.

Soames, Emma (2021) *Mary Churchill's War: The Wartime Diaries of Churchill's Youngest Daughter,* Two Roads, London.

Stevenson, D.E. (2013) *The Two Mrs Abbotts*, Persephone Books Ltd. (first published 1943, Collins)

Sweet, Matthew (2011) *West End Front,* Faber & Faber, London.

Taggart, Caroline (2019) *Wartime Summer: true stories of love, life and loss on the British Home Front,* John Blake Publishing Ltd., London.

Williams, Sir Herbert (1949) *Politics—Grave and Gay*, Hutchinson & Co, Ltd.

Williams, Sir Herbert, correspondence with Lord Beaverbrook, Parliamentary Archives, BBK C/324 and C/325.

Williams, Sir Herbert, *The Week in Westminster,* 22 April 1944, BBC Home Service, London. p.4, BBC Archives.

Wolff-Monckeberg, Mathilde (2007) *On the Other Side: Letters to my children from Germany 1940–46*, Persephone Books, London.

Ziegler, Philip (2002) *London at War 1939–1945,* Pimlico, London.

Zwitter, Cohen, Barrett & Robinton (2002) 'Dorothy Reed and Hodgkin's Disease: a reflection after a century', *International Journal* of *Radiation Oncology Biological Physics, Vol. 53, No. 2,* pp.366–375, Elsevier Science Inc.

V-weapons

Books

Bates, H.E., edited Bob Ogley (1994) *Flying Bombs over England,* Froglets Publications, Kent.

Campbell, Christy (2012) *Target London: Under attack from the V-weapons during WWII,* Little, Brown, London.

Carmichael, Jane (2004) *The V-weapons campaign against Britain 1944–45,* Imperial War Museum.

Clapson, Mark (2019) *The Blitz Companion.* pp.37–75. London: University of Westminster Press. DOI: https://doi.org/10.16997/book26.c. https://www.jstor.org/stable/j.ctvggx2r2.9

Courageous Croydon (1984) Croydon Advertiser Group of Newspapers, Croydon.

Flint, Peter and Iris (1994) *Bourne doodlebugs: North East Surrey and the flying bombs,* The Bourne Society, http://bournesoc.org.uk/

Fry, Helen (2019) *The walls have ears,* Yale University Press, New Haven and London.

Hastings, Max (2016) *The Secret War: Spies, Codes and Guerrillas 1939–1945,* Collins, London.

Hemming, Henry (2017) *M: Maxwell Knight, MI5's Greatest Spymaster,* Penguin, London.

Hesketh, Roger (1999) *Fortitude: the D-Day Deception Campaign,* St Ermin's Press/Little, Brown, London.

Howard, Michael (1990) *British Intelligence in the Second World War, vol. 5, Strategic Deception,* London, HMSO.

Irons, Roy (2002) *Hitler's Terror Weapons: the price of vengeance,* Harper Collins, London.

Irving, David (1985) *The Mare's Nest,* Panther Books, London.

Jeffery, Keith (2010) *MI6: The history of the secret intelligence service 1909–1949,* Bloomsbury, London.

Longmate, Norman (1981) *The doodlebugs: the dramatic story of the flying bombs of World War II,* Arrow Books Ltd., London.

MacIntyre, Ben (2015) *All fair in war: a history of military deception,* BBC Sounds, London.

MacIntyre, Ben (2012) *Double Cross,* Bloomsbury, London.

Masterman, J.C. (1972, 2013) *The double-cross system,* Vintage Books, London.

Rankin, Nicholas (2008) *Churchill's wizards: the British genius for deception 1914–1945,* Faber and Faber, London.

Smith, Peter J.C. (2006) *Air-Launched Doodlebugs: the forgotten campaign,* Pen and Sword Aviation, Barnsley, South Yorkshire.

Thomas, Graham A (2008, 2020) *Hitler's terror from the sky: the battle against the flying bombs,* Pen & Sword Aviation, Barnsley, Yorkshire.

Wybrow, Robert J (1989) *Britain speaks out, 1937–87,* MacMillan Press Ltd, Basingstoke.

Young, Richard Anthony (1978) *The flying bomb,* Ian Allan, London.

Zaloga, Steven (2005), *V-1 Flying Bomb 1942–52: Hitler's infamous doodlebug*, Osprey Publishing, Oxford.

Articles/Websites

Bell, R.C. (1944) 'An Analysis Of 259 Of The Recent Flying-Bomb Casualties,' *The British Medical Journal, Vol. 2, No. 4377* (Nov. 25, 1944), pp.689–692.

https://www.jstor.org/stable/20346995

Browne, Ger (2019) *Clare in World War Two – The Emergency – Alphabetical List*, https://www.clarelibrary.ie/eolas/coclare/history/Clare_Emergency_Stories.pdf

Chapman, Terry (n.d.) *The V Weapons Campaign Against Britain, 1944–1945,* Imperial War Museum, London.

Commonwealth War Graves Commission. https://www.cwgc.org/

Eicholz, Enid (1944) 'Londoners and the flying bomb', *Social Work (1939–1970),* Vol. 3, No. 4 (October 1944), pp. 91-95. Oxford University Press. https://www.jstor.org/stable/43759790

Emrich, Duncan (1945) 'Flying Bomb Folklore,' *California Folklore Quarterly*, Vol. 4, No. 1 (Jan. 1945), pp.76-81. Western States Folklore Society. https://www.jstor.org/stable/1495458

Evans, Stephen G and Delaney, Keith B (2018) 'The V1 (Flying Bomb) attack on London (1944–1945); the applied geography of early cruise missile accuracy'.

Applied Geography 99 (2018) pp.44–53. https://doi.org/10.1016

Jones, Edgar, Woolven, Robin, Durodie, Bill and Wessely, Simon (2004) 'Civilian Morale during the Second World War: Responses to Air Raids Re-examined,' *Social History of Medicine,* vol.17 No. 3.

Kennedy, Dominic. "How agents saved London from Nazi doodlebugs." *The Times,* 30 Mar. 2002, p.22. The Times Digital Archive, https://link.gale.com/apps/doc/IF0501488837/GDCS.

Irving, David (1964) 'Who Are We to Act as God?' *Sunday Telegraph,* 15 Nov. 1964, p.4

Shaw, Liam P. & Luke F (2019) 'The flying bomb and the actuary,' *Significance Magazine,* Wiley & Sons Inc. https://doi.org/10.1111/j.1740-9713.2019.01315.x

Tavares Jr, Major Ernest S., (2001) *Operation Fortitude: the closed loop D-day deception plan,* Air University, Alabama.

Woolven, Robin (2002) 'London and the V weapons 1943–1945', *The RUSI Journal,* 147:1, pp.53–59, DOI: 10.1080/03071840208446741

WWII Letters to Wilma (Fourth Child) https://wwii-letters-to-wilma.blogspot.com/

Zwitter, M., Cohen, J., et al, *Dorothy Reed and Hodgkin's disease: a reflection after a century,* Int. J. Radiation Oncology Biol. Phys., Vol. 53, No. 2, pp.366–375, 2002.

Scotland

ADS, Defence of Britain: https://archaeologydataservice.ac.uk/archives/view/dob/download.cfm

Campsie, Alison (2020) 'The long summer when 2,300 Russian sailors anchored in the Firth of Forth', *The Scotsman,* 19 July 2020.

https://www.scotsman.com/heritage-and-retro/heritage/long-summer-when-2300-russian-sailors-anchored-firth-forth-2917474

Shennon, Rhona (2019) 'Fortitude North: the story of the fictional Scottish army that tricked the Nazis before D-Day,' *The Scotsman*, 3 June 2019.

https://www.scotsman.com/whats-on/arts-and-entertainment/fortitude-north-story-fictional-scottish-army-tricked-nazis-d-day-1416247.

Budleigh Salterton and Exmouth

Berry, Les and Gosling, Gerald (1998) *Budleigh Salterton and Raleigh Country,* Nonsuch, Stroud, Glocs.

Cook, Arthur (2010) *Exmouth at War,* Halsgrove, Wellington, Somerset.

Delderfield, Eric R. (1948) *Exmouth Milestones: a history,* ERD Publications, Devon.

Delderfield, R.F. (1951) *Nobody Shouted Author,* Werner Laurie, London.

Dennys, Joyce (1986) *Henrietta Sees It Through,* Andre Deutsch, London.

Dennys, Joyce (1983) *And Then There Was One,* Tabb House, Cornwall.

Erikson, Yvonne (no date) *Frewins: the history of a road,* Devon Library & Information Services, Exeter.

(No author) *Exmouth: a guide to Budleigh Salterton and the south Devon coast* (no date), Ward Lock & Co Ltd., London and Melbourne.

Fairlynch Museum, Budleigh Salterton (no date) *Salterton at War: the Second World War, Book Two,* File held in museum.

Gibson, F. Tregarthen (2003) *Exmouth: her age of elegance,* Halsgrove, Wellington, Somerset.

Gooding, Jim (1987) *Budleigh Salterton in Bygone Days,* Devon Books, Devon County Library Service, Exeter.

Hoskins, W.G. (1972) *Devon,* David & Charles, Newton Abbot, Devon.

Loman, Nick (2018) *Budleigh at War: a first-hand account of wartime life in Budleigh Salterton,* DVD ©Nick Loman.

Loman, Nick (2018) *Wartime memories of Budleigh Salterton residents,* DVD ©Nick Loman.

Maxted, Ian (ed) (1995) *Devon's testimony of war,* Wheaton Publishers, Exeter.

The Budleigh Salterton, Knowle and East Budleigh Street Directory and Gazetteer for 1947, printed and published by W.J. Delderfield and Sons Ltd., Exmouth, Devon.

Wesley, Kenneth [no date] *Somewhere Over the Rainbow,* [unpublished]. Held at Fairlynch Resource Centre, Budleigh Salterton.

Wolmar, Christian (2020) *Cathedrals of steam,* Atlantic Books, London.

Purley

Harper, Charles G. (1902) *Cycle rides round London,* Chapman and Hall, London.

Higham, A. (ed) (1996) *Purley (No. 1 Village Histories)* The Bourne
Society, Purley.

Acknowledgements

I am grateful to the following for their help in the preparation of this book:

Steve Hunnisett, @Blitzwalker, https://blitzwalkers.blogspot.com/

Stephen Henden http://flyingbombsandrockets.com/index.html

Neil Quinn, Croydon at War: https://www.facebook.com/groups/2273858826254974

Tony Tickner, Croydon and Surrounding Areas History Group: https://www.facebook.com/groups/189408131212693

Lindsay Ould, borough archivist, Croydon

Edward Petrie-Smith, local historian, Croydon

Laurence Spring, Surrey History Centre

The Bourne Society: http://bournesoc.org.uk/

Roz Hickman, Fairlynch Museum and Archive, Budleigh Salterton

Nick Loman, local historian, Budleigh Salterton

Michael Downes, Budleigh Past and Present: https://www.facebook.com/groups/1263602983802611/

Claire Lucas, Museum Manager, Rustington Museum, West Sussex.

Cate Allison, archivist (WAC Catalogue), Archives Technology & Services,

BBC Written Archives Centre, Caversham.

Gordon Barclay, historian, https://gordon-barclay.net/

Dr Joyce E.M. Steele, FSA Scot, curator, The Royal Highland Fusiliers Museum

Staff at Bridport Public Library, The London Library, The National Archives and

The Parliamentary Archives.

His Honour Patrick Moloney QC for advice on the Rustington Trespass Case,

Dr Adrian Clarke for advice on Hodgkin's Disease and TB,

Sabine Schadschneider for translating Otto's letters,

Sylvia Suddes for copy editing, Any errors are mine, not hers.

Kathleen Ferry, Elaine Cain, Deirdre Hyde and Sarah Oram for advice and comments,

Ray Stamford for his support and encouragement.

The photograph of the V1 on the front cover is copyright of the Imperial War Museum and is reproduced with permission.

[1] Ziegler, p.253

[2] Vere Hodgson, p.466

[3] TNA, WO199/2862

[4] ibid.

[5] TNA, WO199/2854

[6] TNA, WO199/2863, Doc. 168

[7] *Croydon Advertiser,* 30 January 1939, p.8

1 [8]The band was probably playing at the bandstand in the Purley Rotary Field on the Brighton Road. The Golden Wheel is long gone.

2 [9] First broadcast in November 1929, the programme was still running in 2023, albeit in a different format.

[10] Williams, *The Week in Westminster,* 22 April 1944, p.4, BBC Archives

[11] HC Deb, 25 April 1944, vol. 399 cc618–9

[12] HC Deb, 25 April 1944, vol. 399 cc623–4

[13] HC Deb, 26 April 1944, vol. 399 cc885–93

[14] HC Deb, 27 April 1944, vol. 399 cc916–7

[15] TNA WO199/2864

[16] TNA WO199/2864 Doc. 153

3 [17]Oliver's birthday party would have taken place in mid-March, while Clem was on leave.

[18] TNA WO199/2848 7 June 1944

[19] TNA WO199/2841 27 May 1944

[20] *The Times,* 13 June 1944, p.4

[21] Bates, p.121

4 [22]The men were later filmed by Pathe for their newsreel *Front Line London.*

[23] Campbell, p.250

[24] Irving, p.189–90

[25] Carmichael, p.1

[26] Lownie, p.118

[27] Gardiner, p.548

[28] *Croydon Times*, 24 June 1944

[29] HC Deb, 16 June 1944, vol. 400 cc2301–3

5 [30]'Getting the wind up' is a pejorative phrase that arose during the First World War and was applied to soldiers whose resilience was deemed to be 'weak' and lacking in 'moral fibre'.

[31] Campbell, p.245

[32] TNA, KV-2-69-66, 16th June 1944

[33] Masterman, p.165

[34] TNA, KV 2/40 18 July 1944

[35] *Courageous Croydon,* p.19

[36] http://www.westendatwar.org.uk/ Bomb Incidents – Guards' Chapel. Quoted by Brell Ewart on 10/10/2020

[37] TNA, KV-2-69-66, 18 June 1944.

[38] Irving, p.190

[39]   https://www.ww2civildefence.co.uk/blog/british-pathe-fim-bomb-damage-london-1944

[40] *The Times,* 21 June 1944, p.2

[41] Bates, p.42

5.1 [42] Clapson, p.73

[43] *Daily Telegraph,* 31 June 1944, p.8

[44] *Courageous Croydon,* p.34

[45] *Courageous Croydon,* p.41

[46] *Croydon Times,* 8 July 1944

[47] *The Manchester Guardian* (1901–1959); 8 July 1944, p.7

[48] *Croydon Times,* 8 July 1944

[49] HC Deb, 23 June 1944, vol. 401 cc482–8

[50] TNA, CAB 66/51/43

[51] *Croydon Times,* 8 July 1944

[52] *Courageous Croydon,* p.32

6 [53]Steel-framed 'cages' set up indoors in which people could sleep. During the day the top could be used as a table.

[54] *Courageous Croydon,* p.40

[55] *Courageous Croydon,* p.28

[56] Emrich, p.78.

[57] TNA, CAB 65-42-42

[58] HC Deb, 29 June 1944, vol. 401 cc788–90

[59] HC Deb, 29 June 1944, vol. 401 cc799–800

[60] Longmate, p.184

[61] *Picture Post,* 1 July 1944, p.12

[62] *Daily Mirror,* 23 August 1944 Bareham later remarried and lived in the street until his death in 1972.

[63] https://www.historynet.com/sloane-court.htm

[64] HC Deb, 4 July 1944, vol. 401 c986

[65] HC Deb, 4 July 1944, vol. 401 cc996–8

[66] Morrison, p.194

[67] HC Deb, 6 July 1944, vol. 401 cc1322–39

[68] *The Times,* 7 July 1944, p.8

[69] HC Deb, 7 July 1944 vol. 401 cc1429–32

[70] HC Deb, 14 July 1944, vol. 401 cc2008–10

[71] *Courageous Croydon,* p.39

[72] *Daily Telegraph,* 10 July 1944, p.5

7 [73] Levis 'discovered' Barry Took and Jim Dale, although in 1957 he turned down a skiffle group called The Quarrymen who later became The Beatles.

8 [74] Boot's the Chemist used to run its own private library, generally considered more acceptable to the middle classes than public libraries. Yvonne belonged to both.

[75] Shennon

[76] Howard, p.191

[77] Campsie

[78] TNA, WO199/2864, 17 July 1944

[79] TNA, WO199/2848, 28 July 1944

[80] Campbell, p.358

[81] TNA, CAB 80 85,_2 Crossbow Deception Policy – Note by Sir Findlater Stewart

[82] TNA, COS (44), 680 (0), 31 July 1944

[83] Irving, 1964

[84] Longmate, p.377

[85] Longmate, p. 379

9 [86] HC Deb 20 July 1944 vol 402 cc327-8

10 [87]Mary Nicholson's husband was Captain John R.A. Nicholson of the 1st Battalion Leicestershire Regiment. They married in October 1939 in Aldershot; he died, aged 32, in the fighting near Caen.

[88] Bell, p.689

[89] Vere Hodgson, p.504

[90] Campbell, p. 345

[91] *Croydon Times,* 29 July 1944, front page

[92] *Evening Despatch,* 29 July 1944, front page

11 [93]The family leased Foxley Lodge.

[94] Gilbert, Jos(eph), Geo(rge), 1944, *Shine on Victory Moon,* Bevan Music Productions Ltd

[95] Delderfield, p.26

[96] 1931 Census of England and Wales, *Occupation Tables*, Budleigh Salterton, Table 17 https://www.visionofbritain.org.uk/

[97] Loman, p.2

12 [98]This would have been at the branch of the National Provincial in the High Street, now a café.

13 [99] Presumably divorced because Rhoda Bevan lived until 1933.

[100] *Daily Mail,* 14 August 1944

[101] *Daily Mail,* 19 August 1944

[102] *West Sussex Gazette,* 31 August 1944

[103] *The Times,* 8 September 1944, p.8

[104] *Croydon Times,* 10 September 1944

[105] *Croydon Times,* 14 October 1944

[106] *Daily Mail* 6 September 1944

[107] TNA, CAB 65-43-34, 7 September 1944

[108] Ziegler, p.302

[109] ibid

[110] *Croydon Times*, 30 September 1944, p.5

[111] https://www.nasa.gov/topics/history/features/vonbraun.html

[112] Collingham, p.157

[113] WWII V2 Rocket Attacks, https://www.wrsonline.co.uk/big-ben-rocket-strikes/1944-v2-rocket-attacks-map/

[114] TNA, HO 2818/14/16, Supplementary Blitz papers

[115] TNA, WO199/2862 Doc. 92

[116] TNA, WO199/2860 Doc. 230

[117] TNA, WO199/2864, Doc. 192

1.1 [118] Smith, p.107

[119] *Courageous Croydon*, p.43

[120] Vere Hodgson, p.539.

[121] HC Deb, 10 November 1944, vol. 404 cc1653–4

[122] *Daily Mail,* 11 Nov. 1944

[123] Chisholm & Davie, p.391

[124] Surrey Mirror and County Post, 8 Nov 1940

[125] Hansard, 5 December 1944, Co mons, Oral Answers to Questions

[126] *Devon and Exeter Gazette,* 16 Feb 1945, p.5

[127] *The Times,* 23 December 1944, p.2

14 [128]Mistaken rumour. All reports mention the saucepans and it is unlikely that ice creams would be so popular in November.

15 [129]Smith, p.156

[130] *Croydon Times,* 23 December 1944

[131] *The Times,* 30 December 1944

[132] Colville, *Fringes of Power,* p.550, quoted in Jenkins, p.773

[133] https://der-fuehrer.org/reden/english/45-01-01.htm

[134] *Devon and Exeter Gazette,* 5 January 1945

16 [135] The hotel in Stirling where Clem was billeted

[136] Campbell, p.420

[137] ibid

17 [138] Slang for a barrage balloon, so in this case a 'windbag' or a pompous old fool.

18 [139] Antwerp suffered 10,145 casualties from a bombardment of 628 V1s and 453 V2s. British newspapers reported very little about this, partly so as not to affect morale but also, again, to prevent the Germans from knowing where they were landing.

[140] Campbell, p.412

[141] https://en.wikipedia.org/wiki/Bezuidenhout

[142] Margaret Cotton, 8 Mar 1945, IWM Dept of Documents 93/3/1 p.39, quoted in Gardiner, p.541.

[143]   IWM   https://www.iwm.org.uk/history/the-terrifying-german-revenge-weapons-of-the-second-world-war

[144] ibid

[145] Campbell, p.445

[146] *Croydon News,* 23 September 1944

[147] Campbell p.445.

[148] Edgerton, p.285

[149] Collingwood, p.468

[150] Commonwealth War Graves Commission (2014-05-11). Annual Report 2013-2014. issuu p.43.

[151] Edgerton, p.285, quoting Ministry of Information *What has Britain done?* p.66

[152] Wikipedia https://en.wikipedia.org/wiki/World_War_II_casualties

[153] *Sunday Telegraph*, 15 Nov. 1964, p. 4+

[154] Young, p.74

[155] Howard, p.177

[156] Bates, p.61

[157] *The Times,* 23 June 1982, p.12

[158] Vere Hodgson, p.568

[159] Information provided by Head of Local History, Fairlynch Museum, Budleigh Salterton.

    19 [160]Based on Wesley.

20 [161] Not traced

21 [162] Probably in Exmouth

[163] Morrison, p.240

[164] *The Yorkshire Observer,* 5 July 1945, front page

[165] *Lewisham Borough News,* 10 July 1945, front page and p.5

[166] Williams, p.145

22 [167] I've seen Sherbrook Hill: the thought is terrifying.

[168] Cyril Raymond, who played the husband, served in the RAF during the Battle of Britain as a fighter controller at Kenley aerodrome, a couple of miles from Dale Road.

[169] *The Western Morning News,* 19 July 1945, p.2

[170] *Devon and Exeter Gazette,* 13 July 1945

[171] Lewisohn, p.254

[172] Rifkind, Hugo, *The Times,* Saturday May 14 2022, p.7

[173] The house was still a dental surgery in 2023.

[174] Zwitter et al, p.371

[175] Parliamentary Archives, BBK C/324

About the Author

Sarah worked as a secretary in London during the 1970s. Her diary for 1971 was published by Collins in 2016 as *The secret diary of a 1970s secretary* and was followed by *Short Skirts and Shorthand: Secretaries of the 1970s*.

She subsequently qualified as a librarian and worked in both public and academic libraries..

Read more at https://sarahshawwords.blogspot.com/.